LIVING
THE LECTIONARY

LIVING
THE LECTIONARY
LINKS TO LIFE AND LITERATURE

YEAR C

GEOFF WOOD

LITURGY
TRAINING
PUBLICATIONS

Acknowledgments

We are grateful to the many publishers and authors who have given permission to include their work. Every effort has been made to determine the ownership of all texts and to make proper arrangements for their use. We will gladly correct in future editions any oversight or error that is brought to our attention.

Excerpts from the poetry of Emily Dickinson are reprinted with permission of the publishers and Trustees of Amherst College from *The Poems of Emily Dickinson,* Thomas H. Johnson, ed., Cambridge, Massachusetts: The Belknap Press of Harvard University Press, copyright © 1951, 1955, 1979 by the President and Fellows of Harvard College.

Excerpt from "You Can Tell the World" (p. 10), new words and new music adaptation by Bob Campbell and Bob Gibson, TRO, copyright © 1961 (renewed), 1958 (renewed), 1969 (renewed) Melody Trails, Inc., The Richmond Organization, 266 West Thirty-seventh Street, New York, New York 10018.

"Silence" (pp. 99–100) by R. S. Thomas from *No Truce with the Furies,* Bloodaxe Books, 1995. Reprinted with permission.

LIVING THE LECTIONARY: LINKS TO LIFE AND LITERATURE, YEAR C © 2003 Archdiocese of Chicago: Liturgy Training Publications, 1800 North Hermitage Avenue, Chicago IL 60622-1101; 1-800-933-1800, fax 1-800-933-7094, e-mail orders@ltp.org. All rights reserved. See our website at www.ltp.org.

This book was edited by Margaret M. Brennan. Kris Fankhouser was the production editor. The design is by Anna Manhart, and the typesetting was done by Kari Nicholls in Minion.

Printed in the United States of America.

Library of Congress Control Number: 2003106867

ISBN 1-56854-365-4

LIVLC

Contents

Wrapped in the Word: An Introduction

Last Sunday I spent a long time looking at the large baptismal font near the front doors of my parish church, St. Augustine's in Washington, D.C. I stared at the steps that could be seen through the water and thought of all who had descended them—infants, children, adults— for immersion in baptismal waters. They had come to that first step, I realized, through human influences, but also very often because of a biblical story, poetry, or prophecy that called them to new life. On leaving the pool, they had joined their newfound friends for a meal at the sacred table and continue to be fed, throughout their days, by the eucharist and the word, that is, by story, poetry, and prophecy.

Geoff Wood in *Living the Lectionary: Links to Life and Literature* does something few authors have done: In each essay he focuses on a story, poem, or prophecy from the Sunday lectionary readings and then links it to a story or poem from the broader world of literature or to life experience. We do not hear the scriptural commentator's voice, though the author knows the Bible well, but rather the voice of someone who loves literature, loves the Bible, and can't contain himself in the playful exercise of finding connections between the two.

Here's how it works: For the First Sunday of Advent we are invited to remember the familiar. We live in hope—Snow White for the coming of her prince, Briar Rose for her prince, and of course the Frog Prince for his princess. These were our childhood friends, possibly exerting more power over our imaginations than characters from novels but also preparing us for them. Next, F. Scott Fitzgerald's *The Great Gatsby* is projected onto our screen. Jay Gatsby, who lives in constant hope that Daisy will be his wife, extends his arms "toward the green light across the water that glows in front of [her] mansion." "The future," Gatsby says, ". . . recedes before us . . . but that's no matter— tomorrow we will run faster, stretch out our arms farther. . . . And one fine morning. . . ." Next we hear an echo from the day's first reading, Jeremiah 33:14–15: "The days are coming when all God's promises will be fulfilled. A fresh branch will surely sprout from the seemingly dead tree of Judah."

The connection has been made, but the job is only half done. "What expectation marks this Advent season for Christians?" asks our guide at these intersecting roads. Meditation seems to be the order of the day—not explication, not exhortation. "We will know of Christ's arrival," says the author (with a conviction that comes, I would suspect, from years of prayer and listening) "when the words that begin to come out of our mouths are healing words and our touch a magic touch; when [our] world begins to look like a . . . Promised Land at last, simply because our once timid, passive eyes now share Christ's own vision of the universe."

In the essay for the Ninth Sunday in Ordinary Time, Willa Cather's *My Ántonia* has us traveling at high speed from the French Catholic parish of Sainte-Agnes in 1890 Nebraska to a Temple and a Gate called Beautiful, through which in the Acts of the Apostles a lame man, leaping and praising God, follows Peter. From this Gate we're projected into our own parishes, "which after all is what they are supposed to be: gateways to a world called Beautiful."

A much more leisurely approach is reflected in the essay for the Fifteenth Sunday in Ordinary Time, where we explore the film *Wrestling Ernest Hemingway*. Slowly, gracefully, and with great care, a retired Cuban-American barber (played by Robert Duvall) cuts the hair of his loud and boisterous friend, played by Richard Harris. The grace and beauty of Duvall's movements ("an ordinary deed turned into a quiet ballet") stay with us long after the tale is told. The corresponding story from the gospels—are we surprised?— is the parable of the Good Samaritan.

Playful, marvelous, joy-filled: Wood uses those words to describe God's word, but in the next breath he will say that the word is a difficult guest once invited into the heart.

He would have no argument with the poem prayer from *The Desert Is Fertile* (Orbis Books, 1981) by the late Dom Helder Camara:

Take away the quietness
of a clear conscience,
Press us uncomfortably.
For only thus
that other peace is made,
your peace.

The "pressing"—to use Helder Camara's image—is barely noticeable in these essays, but more like Jesus' oft-quoted yoke. But be ready for surprises: not the kind that contradict something you've known all your life but the kind that affirm the familiar, something you've chosen not to look at for fear perhaps of identity loss. I was not ready, for example, for the meditation offered in the Sixth Sunday in Ordinary Time. The readings were Jeremiah 17:5–8 and Luke 6:17, 20–26; the related novel was George Eliot's *Middlemarch.* I perceived nothing threatening at first—the likable, young Fred Vincy obviously has nothing to do with me: He is irresponsible and unreliable; he gambles, impoverishes a family to save himself and cares only about his own image. Then comes the jolt: "It dawns on me," writes Wood, "that Jesus would liberate me from my incarceration in a universe inhabited by myself alone. And first of all he would entice me simply to notice other people, to take in their features." "Take in their features?" I ask myself, "I never notice features." Then the whisper: "Fred Vincy, you and I have more in common than I first thought."

The book is for everybody—for those who crave good images and good stories; for those who find their identity in baptism and eucharist and cannot imagine a life without the warmth of good worship; for those who need to laugh, especially at themselves; and, above all, for those who want to wrap themselves in the word, Sunday after Sunday.

I discovered a lovely tale the other day that appears on a pillar in the Holocaust Memorial at Quincy Market in Boston. Ilse, a six-year-old and friend of Guerda Weissman Kline in Auschwitz, finds a raspberry in the camp. She carries it with her all day in her pocket and at night, with eyes shining, gives it to Guerda on a leaf. "Imagine a world," writes Guerda years later, "in which your entire possession is one raspberry, and you give it to your friend" (Rosamond Stone Zander and Benjamin Zander, *The Art of Possibility* [Boston: Harvard Business School Press, 2000], 90).

When I finished the story, I unconsciously started to recall particular psalms—then laments—that would complement it. Then I checked to make sure that my choice appears in the lectionary. I seem to be doing the work of the author! And I think he would be delighted!

Virginia Sloyan

FIRST SUNDAY OF ADVENT

Jeremiah 33:14–16, Luke 21:25–36, F. Scott Fitzgerald

Objects in This Mirror . . .

"Someday my prince will come," sings Snow White. And then there's that other sleeping beauty, Briar Rose, waiting for her prince to come—and the Frog Prince waiting for his princess to come.

And there's Jay Gatsby (in F. Scott Fitzgerald's novel *The Great Gatsby*) stretching out his arms toward the green light across the water that glows in front of Daisy Buchanan's mansion, the Daisy with whom he hopes to live happily ever after. In so many ways we human beings are creatures of expectation. The future "year by year recedes before us," says the novel's narrator, ". . . But that's no matter—tomorrow we will run faster, stretch out our arms farther . . . And one fine morning. . . ."[1]

Students of our culture think that this element of expectation, this hope that someday our current emptiness will give way to fulfillment, is traceable to our biblical heritage. Ever since God called Abraham and told him to "set out for the land I will show you," the people of Israel have been a questing people, ever en route from an oppressive Egypt to some Promised Land where they would finally experience fullness of life. And even though that Promised Land kept eluding them, they held its image before them.

The prophecies we read throughout Advent echo something of that expectation: The days are coming when all God's promises will be fulfilled. A fresh branch will surely sprout from the seemingly dead tree of Judah. Lay aside your mourning clothes, O Jerusalem; dress up for the coming day. And the momentum of it all spills over into other New Testament readings where we hear John the Baptist repeat the words of Isaiah, "In the desert prepare the way of the Lord!" (Isaiah 40:3), and Luke tells us, "Stand . . . raise your heads . . . your redemption is at hand!" (Luke 21:28).

Skeptics must smile at such persistent expectation. "When," they may well ask, "will this prince come? Or can you say he has already come? Did the ancient arrival of Jesus really change much? Look around you, read the newspapers. And even if you give him a second chance, talk about a second coming, when precisely will that be? In the year 3000 or 4000?" They continue, "You say the word Advent means arrival. Arrival of what? A toy infant Jesus to be boxed in January and put away until next year? That is, if some local wags don't run off with it while the town's asleep."

Well, maybe we do have to do some re-evaluation of what all this expectation is about. Does what we're waiting for really lie "out there" in front of us somewhere, in some green light across the bay, some promised land beyond the next horizon? Or, is what we long for something that's gaining on us from behind? Or rather, does it come from within us?

I think a good case can be made for its coming surprisingly from within. In which case, all biblical prophecy may be simply equivalent to the rearview mirror or those mirrors attached to the side of your car. They are situated in front of you, they display an image before your eyes, but in fact they only reflect what's approaching you from behind, from within!

So using this analogy—yes, the Prince is coming! Yes, it's legitimate to expect fulfillment, to long for it. Redemption is indeed at hand, but by way of the presence of Christ and his Spirit unfolding, growing, permeating our minds and hearts and senses from within. And we will know of his arrival when the words that begin to come out of our mouths are healing words and our touch a magic touch; when the world we see around us begins to look like a cosmic garden, a promised land at last, simply because our once timid, passive eyes now share Christ's own vision of the universe.

That may be soon if we are to believe those words inscribed on that side view mirror: "Objects in this mirror are closer than they appear."

FIRST SUNDAY OF ADVENT
TOPICAL: ADVENT

A Miracle Is Nothing More Than The Unexpected!

Once, during the first week of Advent, I had a dream in which I was a eucharistic minister involved in a concelebrated Mass. It's communion time and I am directed toward the communion *rail* (which goes to show how the past and present coalesce in dreams). I hold not a ciborium but a paten (a shallow silver plate) containing five white hosts. The communicants are all Mexican Catholics.

Suddenly the paten I hold begins to widen and the hosts begin to multiply—so rapidly that they are piling up and cascading over the sides of the widening paten! I have to expand the circle of my embrace to keep them from falling to the floor. No sooner do I do that than tiny rosebuds appear amid all that whiteness. My reaction is one of panic but also of excitement because I realize I am witnessing a miracle. Until then miracles had always been something I had read about, something that happened to people 2,000 years ago or to a peasant girl at Lourdes but never to me. Except that here I was with an armful of miracles—that proximate to divine power at work!

I related the dream to my friend Father Aurelio over coffee the next morning and he informed me that the Gospel reading for that weekday's Mass was the multiplication of the loaves. It also occurred to us that the feast of Our Lady of Guadalupe was imminent, with its delightful account of all those roses cascading out of Juan Diego's cloak.

Needless to say, I gave that dream a lot of thought in the context of that Advent season. Advent has to do with the coming of Christ. All through December we read about Hebrew expectations of a final delivery from their oppressors. We hear the prophets pleading with God to intervene in the colossal ways he once did

during the Exodus and at Mount Sinai and during the glorious
reign of King David. They long for a new Exodus, a new Sinai, the
return of David, their Messiah King. And yet at Christmas time
we celebrate the *unexpected* way in which those expectations were
fulfilled—not with fanfare and worldly triumph nor with the
mountains quaking but by way of an infant citizen of Nazareth
(whence people thought no good could come) born amid a caravan
of migrants encamped around Bethlehem's Motel 6.

As we remember Israel's ancient longings for the arrival
of their Messiah, during Advent we also hear in the New Testament
readings of our own longing for Christ's second coming—when
the redemption of the world will be wrapped up once and for all
and how amid fireworks galore, special effects far exceeding the
best Hollywood can offer, the Son of Man will arrive upon clouds
of majesty.

But may we not, like the Hebrews, be so enamored of our
poetic and grandiose expectations of Christ's distant second coming
that we forget: God always comes in *unexpected* ways? Doesn't our
understanding of the Mass tell us over and over again that Christ
comes to us *every* day veiled in bread and wine? I think that's what
that dream was trying to tell me. Christ may very well descend some
day surrounded by angels—but liturgically he prefers to arrive at
the climax of every eucharist we attend. Like the hosts on my paten
he multiplies himself amid an imperceptible fragrance of bloodred
roses; multiplies himself excessively, cascading out of our sanctuaries to make himself one with each of us who, as hosts of Christ,
go cascading back to our pews and out into the world to make of
every day—a Christmas Day—to reveal to all the world that Christ
remains no mere future event but has arrived in his usual unexpected way—in the miracle that is you and I.

SECOND SUNDAY OF ADVENT

Baruch 5:1–9, Herman Melville

Our Annual Return from Exile

There is a poignant chapter in the novel *Moby Dick* in which the good ship Rachel approaches Captain Ahab's whaling ship in the mid-Pacific. Ahab, who is obsessed with finding and killing Moby Dick, calls out, "Hast thou seen the White Whale?" The Rachel's Captain Gardiner replies, "Aye, yesterday." But Captain Gardiner's concern is not over the White Whale but over the disappearance of one of his whaleboats, among whose lost crew is his 12-year-old son. "My boy, my own boy is among them. For God's sake—I beg, I conjure. For eight-and-forty hours let me charter your ship . . . you must, oh, you must, and you shall do this thing." But, as you know, Ahab had no time to help the Rachel find its missing boat as long as Moby Dick lay just over the horizon. And so the Rachel (named for the mother of Israel whose tribes were also lost among the nations) goes on her "halting course and winding, woeful way . . . weeping for her children, because they were not."[2]

There's a similar poignant passage in the biblical book of Baruch. The prophet Baruch writes about a time when the Jewish people were brutally deported from their homeland, to be eventually scattered throughout the Mediterranean world. The author describes Jerusalem as a mother weeping over the disappearance of her children: "Hear, you neighbors of Zion! God has brought great mourning upon me, for I have seen the captivity . . . brought upon my sons and daughters. With joy I fostered them; but with mourning and lament I let them go. Let no one gloat over me, a widow, bereft of many. . . . They have led away this widow's cherished sons, have left me solitary, without daughters. . . . Farewell, my children, farewell" (Baruch 4:9–12, 16, 19).

A boy lost at sea—a sad father. God's people dispersed across the face of the earth—a sad mother. What relevance may they have for us at this season of the year? In my case: much! Every year, with each passing month, I find myself scattered here, there and everywhere. Here's a pressing deadline, there's the latest aggravating headline. Here's the monthly bills, there's the fence needing painting. Here's a ton of e-mail screaming to be answered, there's a book that's a month overdue. Here's a Nike logo and there's a Pepsi logo and here's another phone call in the middle of dinner inquiring whether I'm ready to sell my house. Everywhere around me lies a totally secularized society, bereft of any sense of the sacred. By the time December rolls around, it's like I've spent my whole year in exile—been lost at sea, my mind disoriented, longing to find solace, a home among things that really matter—the meaning of my life.

And so, I thank God for the Christmas season—because every year, when things seem darkest, it awaits us like Jerusalem of old, like a mother expecting our return—ready to gather us within the warmth of Christ's crèche. There (home from exile at last) we may, like Mary, ponder things in our heart and reconnect with our ultimate source and destiny.

And so, let the prophet Baruch of our first reading this Sunday play the herald saying: Jerusalem, take off your robe of mourning and misery. Let him alert mother Jerusalem to our homecoming at last, saying: "Up, Jerusalem! Stand upon the heights; look to the east and see your children gathered from the east and the west. . . . Led away on foot by their enemies they left you: but God will bring them back to you, borne aloft in glory as on royal thrones" (Baruch 5:5–6). Christmas has always been literally considered a time of homecoming. The church would have us understand it to be a time of homecoming in the profoundest sense of the word.

SECOND SUNDAY OF ADVENT
TOPICAL: DIVINE PATIENCE

Charles Dickens, John Galsworthy

Tired of Scrooge? Consider Soames!

Every year as Christmas approaches we revisit the parable of
Ebenezer Scrooge's conversion from a tight-fisted, "squeezing,
wrenching, old sinner" to a man of jolly generosity. We revel in
Dickens's description of him as a man as solitary as an oyster, whose
heart was so cold it froze his features and turned his lips blue—
until, influenced by three spirits, he opened the windows of his soul
to let the sunshine of Christmas in, to experience his own rebirth as
coincidental with that of Christ: "I am as light as a feather, I am as
happy as an angel, I am as merry as a schoolboy."[3] This year, as an
alternative to the monotony of the Scrooge parable, we might look
to the replay of John Galsworthy's *The Forsyte Saga*[4] for a character
quite similar to (if not as comical as) Scrooge, namely Soames
Forsyte, one of the great characters of twentieth-century literature.

Soames is a man of property. Like his father, he spent so
much time "in arranging mortgages, preserving investments . . .
in calculations as to the exact pecuniary possibilities of all the relations of life, he had come at last to think purely in terms of money.
Money was his light, his medium for seeing, that without which he
was really unable to see, really not cognizant of phenomena." He
had become like one of those black holes in space, eager to possess,
reluctant to give. For example, he thought he loved his wife but
actually he valued her as a possession, and he was bewildered over
her aloofness, her refusal to respect him. But what else could she do:
She wanted to be loved, not owned. Alluding to an episode in the
book of Daniel, Galsworthy describes Soames's inability to read
the handwriting on every wall of his house that declared he might

possess her body (if he even possessed that) but he could never own her soul.

And yet Soames was not insensible to the enticements of the Holy Spirit to engage with (instead of consume) the world around him. These enticements did not come in the shape of midnight visits as in the case of Scrooge, but at moments when twice or so a week he would, for no clear reason, enter Saint Paul's Cathedral to wander about. But the only benefit he derived from such visits was a moment of quiet sufficient to focus better upon some business coup! Nevertheless, the Holy Spirit was happy enough to get him over the threshold of a new world. After all, inspiration has to begin somewhere!

And then there was another occasion when Soames was inspired to build a country home far from the stuffy London he preferred. But he wanted the house built on the cheapest lot until his architect insisted it occupy a crest where fields of wheat stretched far away to a grove of trees and larks sang and the grass gave off a fragrance. Immediately Soames recoiled at the possible price of such a view. Yet in spite of himself "something swelled within his breast." It was obviously something within him that wanted to expand rather than possess, that wanted to live, to experience the sacramentality of nature, to reconnect with the source of his being. Once more, however, the Holy Spirit had to be patient, for immediately Soames lapsed into considering how much the possession of such a view might redound to his *credit*.

In Scrooge's case it took only one night to snap him out of his loveless isolation. In Soames's case it will take years. And even by the novel's end the Holy Spirit's efforts will have planted nothing more than a "melancholy craving in his heart." For though "the sun was like enchantment on his face and on the clouds and on the golden birch leaves, and the wind's rustle was so gentle . . . and the sickle of the moon so pale in the sky," Soames felt that all he could ever do was wish and wish but never quite *know* "the beauty and the loving in the world!"

The Holy Spirit, of course, is not to be thwarted by any novel's arbitrary ending of a human saga nor by any failure of our own to emerge from our own biliousness and live with something of the radiance of Christ—which is why Advent comes round again and again to entice us relentlessly us toward visions of a new heaven and a new earth.

THIRD SUNDAY OF ADVENT

Zephaniah 3:14–18a

Shout for Joy, O Daughter Zion!

> Well you can tell the world about this
> You can tell the nation about that
> Tell'em what the master has done
> Tell'em that the Gospel has come
> Tell'em that the victory's been won
> He brought joy, joy, joy, joy, joy, joy,
> Into my heart.[5]

Simon and Garfunkel did a great revival of that African American spiritual back in the 1960s. Thank God we have our African American heritage to remind us occasionally that Christianity is not only about orthodoxy or moral rectitude or apostolic succession or mystical detachment but about JOY. Joy is a lot more than happiness. Joy is what happens when a guy, who feels very unhandsome and incapable of dancing as well as other guys and therefore resigned to being a perpetual wallflower, is approached by a wonderful girl from across the dance floor who looks him firmly in the eye and says, "You know, I like you . . . and want to marry you!"

Joy is what happens to Woody Allen in the movie *Hannah and Her Sisters* as he sits worriedly in a doctor's office waiting for

a brain specialist to return with the results of X-rays regarding
a possible tumor—eventually to hear the fellow casually say, "Well,
there's nothing here after all. Everything looks fine." Woody Allen
quietly takes the down elevator, walks out onto the sidewalk—and
leaps three feet into the air! Or joy is what happens when you've
been interviewed along with several other impressive candidates for
a job and, after five weeks of waiting and escalating tension, the
phone rings and a cheerful voice says, "The job is yours! How soon
can you start?"

Notice how in every case joy amounts to relief from some
prolonged period of tension or depression. And that's why we associate Jesus with joy, because until Jesus came along we had only two
options. We could either be depressed over the fact that there is no
God or only arbitrary gods and therefore no real meaning to life, or
we could be depressed over the fact that there is a God who, as an
unrelenting overseer, expects us to measure up to a million and one
major and minor tenets and regulations or face dire consequences
(a God not unlike any old Caesar we have known).

With Jesus came the revelation of another option (or rather
fact!) that God is not essentially a judge but a God of grace, compassion, mercy; that God is a parent who understands our fears,
who is more grieved than angry over the sordid things our fear
generates and who will persistently seek access to our hearts until
his own graciousness takes sufficient hold to change us into gracious
beings as well—similar to this Jesus who in word and deed was
a manifestation of what true divinity and humanity is all about.

Radical joy more than anything else has got to be the consequence of such a revelation. That's why Christianity began with
a Pentecostal outburst! And that's what we try to experience anew
every Christmas. That's one reason why (at least when I was a kid)
the Christmas tree was not put up until all the children were in
bed on Christmas Eve—so that on Christmas morning they could
experience the thrill of seeing the living room transfigured, the joy
of finding one surprise after another among all those Christmas

wrappings—so that jaded parents could rekindle the joy they once knew before their lives became habitual almost beyond recovery. Christ is about the astounding, almost unbelievable news: that you are boundlessly loved by someone from beyond the boundaries of space and time, yet so intimately by someone who knows and cherishes you far more than you could possibly know and cherish yourself.

> Well my Lord spoke, he spoke to me
> Yes he did, yes he did
> Talkin' about a man from Galilee
> Yes he did, yes he did. . . .
> He brought joy, joy, joy into my heart.

FOURTH SUNDAY OF ADVENT

Luke 1:39–45, Charles Dickens

Let's Have Lots of Room!

" 'Hilli-ho!' cried old Fezziwig, skipping down from the high desk, with wonderful agility. 'Clear away, my lads, and let's have lots of room here.' "

In his *A Christmas Carol*[6] Charles Dickens presents Fezziwig (Ebenezer Scrooge's early employer) as a stout embodiment of the Christmas spirit, something Scrooge and all of us need to recover if we are ever to become fully human. Fezziwig wants room, space to maneuver, to dance, to be! "Clear away! There was nothing they wouldn't have cleared away, or couldn't have cleared away, with old Fezziwig looking on. It was done in a minute. Every movable was packed off, as if it were dismissed from public life for evermore; the floor was swept and watered, the lamps were trimmed, fuel was heaped upon the fire; and the warehouse was as snug, and warm, and dry, and bright a ball-room, as you would desire to see upon a winter's night."

Fezziwig, understanding and supportive of the impact of Christ's arrival upon this world, would therefore transfigure it from warehouse (a place of quid pro quo and hard bargaining and survival of the fittest) to ballroom wherein a repressed and depressed humanity might loosen up, take partners, "hands half round and back again the other way; down the middle and up again; round and round in various stages of affectionate grouping." In other words, experience life as a dance instead of a dirge.

Fezziwig is a man energized by the arrival and gospel of Christ even as John the Baptist in today's gospel reading was energized. John the Baptist in his mother's womb is symbolic of the condition of the whole human race. Like him, we have lived out our history in a kind of womb, unwilling to be fully born, confined by our fear of God and life and an honest relationship with others. Jesus comes with his gospel of faith, hope and love and no sooner does John sense his presence than he gives his mother an almighty kick! He wants at long last to be born, to emerge from his cocoon and engage with God and the world and others creatively, courageously. He wants at long last to live! And so do we all. Christmas is about multiple births, coincidental with the birth of Christ in our midst.

Even in our cynical age the magic, the vital signs of his coming are visible. I took a stroll among the old Victorian and not-so-Victorian houses of the riverfront town of Petaluma last Sunday. It was a gray, chilly day yet the door wreaths and decorated and colorfully lit Christmas trees peeping out of the windows made the whole place seem somehow warm, alive; it made me think of people as not yet bereft of imagination and wonder and playfulness.

It was just as Dickens described it well over a century ago: "There was nothing very cheerful in the climate or the town and yet there was an air of cheerfulness abroad that the clearest summer air and brightest summer sun might have endeavored to diffuse in vain . . . The very gold and silver fish, set forth . . . in a bowl, though members of a dull and stagnant-blooded race, appeared to know that there was something going on; and, to a fish, went gasping round and round their little world in slow and passionless excitement."

Which goes to show there's hope even for those rationalists (who want to do away with Santa Claus) and for Scrooge and all those other cold fish who would reduce Christmas to a bland celebration of (at most) the winter solstice. Don't tell me they don't feel at least a little something, a bit of stirring, like Elizabeth, within their gut when they, too, hear a Handel chorale trumpeting, "Wonderful, Counsellor, the mighty God, the everlasting Father, the Prince of Peace!"

FOURTH SUNDAY OF ADVENT
TOPICAL: CHRISTMAS

Willa Cather

Nebraska in Winter!

"The first snowfall came early in December. I remember how the world looked from our sitting room window as I dressed behind the stove that morning: the low sky was like a sheet of metal; the blond cornfields had faded out into a ghostliness at last; the little pond was frozen under its stiff willow bushes. Big white flakes were whirling over everything." Winter on the still wild prairie of Nebraska in the 1890s as seen by a boy named Jim Burden in Willa Cather's *My Ántonia!*[7]

Jim lived with his grandparents who with two hired hands, Otto and Jake, managed a farm on what seemed to Jim to be the outer rim of the known world. All summer and fall the family and Otto and Jake worked hard cultivating, harvesting, caring for livestock, storing up for winter. And now it had arrived, the snow so

deep at times that no one could exit their half underground homestead except to see to the stabled horses and cows. "The basement
kitchen seemed heavenly safe and warm in those days—like a tight
little boat in a winter sea. Next to getting warm and keeping warm,
dinner and supper were the most interesting things to think about.
Our lives centered around warmth and food."

In the evening they would sometimes pop corn and make
taffy and Otto would sing "O Bury Me Not On the Lone Prairie."
On other bitter nights as they sat around the stove they could hear
coyotes down by the corral and then Otto and Jake would tell chilling stories about wolves, bears and outlaws they had met—and
funny tales as well.

Christmas was an especially welcome time. Unable to get
to town, the family made its own presents and put up a cedar tree
that grandmother and Otto decorated with gingerbread animals,
strings of popcorn, bits of candle and some old German paper
figures—a heart, the three wise men, a baby in a manger—so that
the tree became "the talking tree of the fairy tale; legends and stories
nestled like birds in its branches." Then on Christmas day grandfather would read solemnly from Matthew's story of the birth of
Christ and lead them in prayer. He led them in prayer too one day
at the burial of a neighbor who died that winter of despair; while
Otto led the mourners through that old hymn:

> Jesus, lover of my soul
> Let me to thy bosom fly
> While the nearer waters role
> While the tempest still is high.

Nebraska in winter! But was that all Willa Cather had in
mind when she wrote her story? I think maybe she had all of us
in mind, too, who live beneath the transparent ceiling of this homestead we call earth, situated in the midst of that other cold and
boundless prairie called the universe. We too live in awe of the

forces of nature out there. We, too, work hard to acquire the food and warmth to delay the mortality that naturally awaits us all.

But Willa Cather makes it clear that food and fire were not all the Burdens depended on to survive. It was their stories, legends, songs, prayers, festivals that kept them alive in a truly human sense— and not like stabled cows and horses! And so it is with us as we ride this planet from whence to who knows where. It is our stories, our gospels, our festivals of Christmas and Easter, our hymns that keep us sane, that nurture our sense of infinite worth and our conviction that we shall live forever! Without those stories, those images, without the spiritual nourishment of celebrations like the eucharist, no matter how full our larder may be, our lives and humanity are empty.

THE NATIVITY OF THE LORD
VIGIL MASS

Isaiah 62:1–5, Mark Twain

For Zion's Sake I Will Not Be Silent

As Huckeberry Finn and his runaway companion, Jim, drifted down the Mississippi one night en route to the Ohio River where Jim might catch a steamboat to the free states, they ran into a thick fog. Huckleberry took a line, got off the raft, and paddled his canoe to a nearby island to tie up the raft for the night. But the current drove the raft with Jim aboard right past the island, so that Huckleberry in the canoe and Jim on the raft became separated, invisible to each other in the fog.

Huckleberry immediately started paddling into the mist in pursuit of the raft but had no idea where he was going; he couldn't see a thing. So he called out. And, as he puts it, "Away down there somewhere I hears a small whoop and I went tearing after it."[8] But the next time he heard it, it seemed to come from the right and then from the left, so that he went flying around this way and the other and getting no nearer. Then he heard a call from behind him. But that sounded not like Jim but somebody else. Still it kept coming and kept changing its place. Finally, Huckleberry gave up, confessing, "I couldn't tell nothing about voices in a fog, for nothing don't look natural or sound natural in a fog."

How well that describes the situation of the human race as it floats upon this planet through space and down the endless river of time, unsure of where we are, whence we've come and where we're going and why. And down through the ages we too have called out; hurled questions into space, prayed to whatever gods might be out there, trying to get some orientation out of the mist and mystery of our existence. And we've heard voices, responses coming from this direction and that—the voices of philosophers and scientists and ideologues and fatalists, all trying to clarify our condition and destiny.

But for all their whooping and hollering, we remain befogged, because all their answers address primarily our intellect; they never address adequately the needs of the heart. For example, for me to be told that we all originate with a Big Bang and have become merely a higher form of animal destined to become extinct along with this planet some day—that's not where my heart wants to arrive! My heart wants to see my children immortal; my heart wants to grow, to discover, to experience reality with ever-greater intensity—not fade into oblivion.

And that's why so many of us discount those futile voices coming to us out of the fog—voices as befogged as we are. That's why I keep turning to catch that other voice that penetrates the mist by way of biblical and biblically influenced storytellers and poets— a voice whose Word lifts the veil to inform us that we are indeed the offspring of a gracious creator whose whole intention is to entice us to risk crossing one horizon after another (even the horizon of death) to become ever more gracious beings ourselves. The Word of God! That's what appeals to the whole human being. And that's a Word that has not only called from beyond the limits of our ignorance but has broken the sound barrier to walk upon the waters, an immortal revelation of what we are destined to become.

How appropriate that we celebrate the arrival of the Word-made-flesh among us at this time of the year. For this is the dark and misty time when we especially need to hear words and experience images that appeal to the heart; when we need consolation and warmth; when we need to hear God shout as he will during the Christmas vigil: "For Zion's sake I will not be silent; for Jerusalem's sake I will not be quiet, until her vindication shines forth like the dawn, and her victory like a burning torch" (Isaiah 62:1).

MASS DURING THE DAY

Isaiah 52:7–10

That Glorious Song of Old

> Old King Cole was a merry old soul,
> And a merry old soul was he.
> He called for his pipe, and he called for his bowl,
> And he called for his fiddlers three.

Not so with old King Saul, the first king of Israel. As he grew older he had little use for music. In fact, music was one of the things he disliked about his popular son-in-law, David, who had this penchant for writing songs (the psalms) and singing them to the accompaniment of a harp and sometimes dancing all night before the ark of the covenant. There's one musical episode reported in the Bible in which Saul became so irked, he threw a spear at David.

And yet music, song, sad songs, songs of joy—these are a very prominent element throughout the Bible. In fact, if you include the book of Psalms, the books of the prophets (which is poetry that can be set to music), the incantations of Balaam and Jacob, the canticles of Moses, Miriam, Hannah, Deborah, the Canticle of Canticles, and so on, close to 50 percent of the Hebrew Scriptures seems to be composed of liturgical music! Why? Because music seemed to be the proper way to address God, and to express one's feelings about God.

A commentator on a recent television special on Italian Americans said "opera" is the way Italians normally speak! Their ordinary conversation is operatic, musical—with vehement lows and ecstatic highs and eloquent gestures. And so it was with the Israelites. You don't mumble when you talk to God; you take a deep breath and speak to him up and down the scale, tenderly, pleadingly, joyfully—depending on how you feel. Music has always been the preferred mode of religious expression, and our very capacity to sing could almost be considered evidence that there is a God!

Look at the role music plays in the story of Christ's birth. Of course, we have Zachary (the father of John the Baptist). He's a bit like King Saul: too wary to believe the angel's message that Elizabeth in her old age could bear a child. You'll notice that Zachary, therefore, remains mute until faith loosens his vocal cords to allow him to sing his magnificent *Benedictus*. But everyone else in the story breaks into song. It's a veritable opera! Elizabeth (whose son dances within her womb), Mary, the angels, the shepherds, Simeon—they all have scores to sing. A great event has occurred, the presence of God has been felt, and music becomes the spontaneous way of expressing joy, wonder, gratitude, and reverence.

I myself am not much of a singer and even less a dancer. You could say I'm shy. Or you could say that, in this regard, my father's cold, northern European genes somehow dominate my mother's Mediterranean genes. And that worries me, because I'm reminded of Jesus' complaint when he couldn't get the scribes to loosen up to savor his Good News: "We piped for you and you would not dance."

So lest I disappoint him, too, I do try to sing more nowadays and will certainly put what I can into bellowing out a few Christmas carols. Should we not all rejoice and sing? For today, a Savior has been born to us!

THE HOLY FAMILY OF JESUS, MARY, AND JOSEPH

Luke 2:41–52, Amy Witting

Post-Christmas Blues

What with Advent expectations and the heightened pressure of Christmas shopping and planning of family reunions, we reach such a peak by December 25 that we've nowhere to go but down, down, down into a funk in the period after Christmas. By December 26 the tree looks old, the gifts under its boughs no longer evoke "oohs" and "aahs," the dishes remain in the washer for want of any will-power to replace them on cabinet shelves and we ask ourselves: Why must Christmas always be but prelude to so profound a state of depression?

Well, to justify your post-Christmas blues, let me give you some serious liturgical and theological reasons why you should indeed be depressed after December 25. Just look at the saints we venerate on the days after Christmas: Stephen, the Holy Innocents, Thomas Becket—martyrs all! Day after day we are confronted with red vestments, symbolic of the blood of people killed for following this infant Jesus. That's enough to cool your Christmas cheer.

Sure, the church wants us to rejoice over the arrival of someone divine in our midst and for that reason selects for the feast itself those more joyful passages from Saint Luke that tell of the Annunciation and of angels singing and shepherds prancing across the hills to Bethlehem. But after Christmas, note how the church shifts into sadder gear, selecting for one liturgical year Luke's later verses about the child's future contradiction and pain, and for this liturgical year Mary's momentary loss of her son at the age of twelve. And only then do we begin to hear passages from Matthew's more ominous account of Christ's birth—with its images of a ruthless Herod and the massacre of infants and the Holy Family's flight into exile.

Christ's birth is indeed something to rejoice over, but it's also an event designed to challenge this insecure, avaricious, cynical, bullheaded, violent world of ours to become Christlike in thought, word, and deed—and the powers that be have little intention of doing that. So you can be sure the Herods of history will continue to pursue this infant Christ of ours relentlessly to crucify and bury him and his absurd gospel of grace to boot. And that's enough to make anyone sad, except that we know that Christ is the most amazing escape artist that's ever been born—a fact indicated in the one birth story we never read at Christmas time.

I refer now to chapter 12 of the book of Revelation, wherein we behold a woman clothed with the sun and on her head a crown of stars. As she is about to give birth, an immense red dragon crouches before her, eager to devour her child. (What truer picture could you imagine of how this world with all its warlike and possessive ways would abort all that Christ stands for.) But upon birth the child is quickly snatched away into heaven, leaving us Christians as leftovers for the dragon to pursue—and if at times we let ourselves be swallowed by him, the least we're required to do is give him indigestion.

So, do you have a case of the post-Christmas blues? Theologically and liturgically speaking, it's the most appropriate (but not hopeless) way to feel, considering the kind of world our newborn Christ must confront, even in the twenty-first century. Still, if it does you any good, why not imitate my Irish dad who, when deeply depressed, relieved himself with a good old Irish curse? And should you be at a loss as to just what kind of curse to utter, you can adopt Amy Witting's potent *A Curse on Herod:*

> May you live forever. In that eternity
> may birdcries from the playground ring in your ear
> incessantly. When you plan your forays, may
> on your terrible blueprints starfish prints appear.

May short fierce arms be locked about your knees
wherever you turn, and small fists drag at your hem
while voices whine of . . . ice cream. These
are your children. You have made them. Care for them.

May you have no rest. May you wake at night with a cry
chilled by a nightmare that you can't dispel.
May the bogeyman be thirty inches high
and immortal. These are you children. Guard them well.[9]

THE EPIPHANY OF THE LORD

William Shakespeare

Twelfth Night

Twelfth Night is one of those Shakespeare plays that pivot around
mistaken identity. In this one a shipwreck separates a young woman
named Viola from her identical twin brother Sebastian. She eventually arrives in the domain of Duke Orsino. Feeling vulnerable, she
disguises herself as a young man and becomes the Duke's courtier.

She is not in the Duke's service for very long before she
begins to fall in love with him, but her male disguise prevents her
from revealing this. The Duke himself, on the other hand, is madly
in love with the Lady Olivia and one day sends our disguised Viola
to Olivia to request her hand in marriage. Olivia declares she can't
stand the Duke, but she does fall head over heels in love with his
messenger, our disguised Viola! And, of course, Viola frantically
resists Olivia's advances.

So because of Viola's deception, we have the following
situation: The Duke loves Olivia, Olivia loves our disguised Viola,
and Viola secretly loves the Duke. Then things get worse:

1. Another fellow, Sir Andrew, also loves Olivia and, resenting her attachment to our disguised Viola, challenges Viola to a duel.

2. In the meantime our disguised Viola's identical twin Sebastian arrives upon the scene.

3. Sir Andrew and friends, thinking Sebastian to be the disguised Viola, assault him, only to get their heads handed to them.

4. Olivia then sees Sebastian and, thinking him to be our disguised Viola, once more pleads with him to marry her.

5. Sebastian, seeing Olivia for the first time and wondering how lucky a fellow can get, accepts her plea (much to Olivia's surprise) and off they go to the chapel.

Now this play was meant to be a comedy, but up to this point, because of Viola's disguise, it could well have turned out to be a tragedy—with an angry duke ready to slay Olivia and banish Viola as a traitorous courtier. But no tragedy occurs because in the end Viola relieves everyone's confusion by revealing her true identity— so that Olivia may now retain Sebastian as her husband, the Duke wed Viola as the woman who truly loves him, and Sebastian and Viola rejoice over the recovery of the twin sibling whom each thought "the blind waves and surges" had devoured.

Shakespeare called this play *Twelfth Night* because it's full of the masquerading and mayhem that occurred at parties held on the eve of Epiphany (which fell on the twelfth night after Christmas). This makes me wonder whether he didn't also intend the play to underscore the very meaning of the Feast of the Epiphany. Think about it: In the play, the chaotic consequences of deception are finally relieved by Viola's "epiphany," her manifestation of her true identity. Now isn't that what the Epiphany of Jesus was meant to achieve? Here we are all caught up in this melodrama called history, a melodrama of disguise, pretense, misunderstanding, and their tragic consequences. And then along comes this Jesus, whose birth was obscure, whose early life hidden, whom we took to be a carpenter's son—and who is finally revealed to be nothing less than the redemptive power of God and Love in our world.

All of which amounts to a summons to each of us to put aside our own disguises by which we confuse the world around us, to reveal that Christic self we have concealed for too long, whose revelation is imperative if we are ever to turn history into a divine comedy after all.

THE BAPTISM OF THE LORD

Luke 3:15–22, Richard Brautigan

Your Catfish Friend

Baptism is as much about immersion, about acquiring a depth dimension as it is about coming up for air. For you really cannot come up for air or ever breathe freely and deeply without having sounded the presence of Christ and God residing at the base of your soul. Once when I was very depressed (and therefore not breathing deeply and freely) a friend sent me a poem by Richard Brautigan that made me go fishing for that presence. It's called "Your Catfish Friend" and it goes like this:

> If I were to live my life
> in catfish forms
> in scaffolds of skin and whiskers
> at the bottom of a pond
> and you were to come by
>   one evening
> when the moon was shining
> down into my dark home
> and stand there at the edge
>   of my affection

and think, "It's beautiful
here by this pond. I wish
            somebody loved me,"
I'd love you and be your catfish
friend and drive such lonely
thoughts from your mind
and suddenly you would be
            at peace,
and ask yourself, "I wonder
if there are any catfish
in this pond? It seems like
a perfect place for them."[10]

May not this whole poem be read on a deeper level as a playful message from Christ himself? And indeed, didn't the early church find in the fish *(ichthys)* a symbol of that Christ whose friendly mission was to lead us into the depths of reality, to make us profound in ways God himself is profound? "Put out into the deep," he once said to his disciples. Get beneath the surface of things. Stop being so shallow when it comes to things like faith, hope, love, and life.

It's shallowness that makes us sad. We know in our heart of hearts that when we are shallow, petty, and taken up with trivial concerns and diversions, we're not realizing the potential we have for a more sublime experience of life. We realize we are wasting our lives and that's what makes us depressed.

But it's precisely then we should remember that deep down within us and beneath the superficialities of this world around us there resides and gracefully moves about a Creator, a friend who is thinking of us and sending up signals of perpetual affection—signals designed to make us think about depth, to make us pause amid our many worries and ask, "I wonder if there are any catfish in this pond. It seems like a perfect place for them."

FIRST SUNDAY OF LENT

Luke 4:1–3, Emily Dickinson

Dialogue in a Desert

There are times when each of us feels adrift in some wasteland (like Jesus in today's gospel): alone, spiritually parched, aimless, with nothing but emptiness and a silent horizon all about us. Emily Dickinson,[11] the nineteenth-century American poet, often felt that way, growing up in a small, Puritan town in Massachusetts. All of her neighbors and friends seemed content with their lives. All the girls in her Mount Holyoke College class, when invited to stand up for Jesus, literally did so at once. Not Emily. She alone remained seated because she just wasn't moved anymore by her Puritan creed, which had degenerated into pulpit platitudes. And she was desolate over it:

> To lose one's faith—surpass
> The loss of an Estate—
> Because Estates can be
> Replenished—faith cannot—
>
> Inherited with Life—
> Belief—but once—can be—
> Annihilate a single clause—
> And Being's—Beggary—
> (#377)

Uncertain of what she believed, hurt and frightened by frequent deaths (death was a very visible event in those days, carrying off the young as much as the old), she sensed she lived within a very fragile circle that could dissolve at any moment into nothingness. To survive this state of mind, she began to write poetry (which is a kind of prayer). To a friend she wrote, "I had a terror—I could tell to none—and so I sing, as the Boy does in the Burying Ground—because I am afraid."

Many of her poems dealt almost despairingly with the death of a friend:

> It tossed—and tossed—
> A little Brig I knew—o'ertook by Blast—
> It spun—and spun—
> And groped delirious, for Morn—
>
> It slipped—and slipped—
> As One that drunken—stept—
> Its white foot tripped—
> Then dropped from sight—
>
> Ah, Brig—Good Night
> To Crew and You
> The Ocean's Heart too smooth—too Blue—
> To break for You—
> (#723)

And many dealt wearily with what she called the "Blank," those ultimate questions about life that science cannot answer:

> From Blank to Blank—
> A Threadless Way
> I pushed Mechanic feet—
> To stop—or perish—or advance—
> Alike indifferent—
> (#761)

But the more she wrote (or prayed), the more she felt the presence of someone beyond the horizon. Her poems became less a monologue and more a dialogue. Even Death became less a chilling event and more a tender visitor, come to escort her home:

> Because I could not stop for Death—
> He kindly stopped for me—
> The Carriage held but just Ourselves—
> And Immortality . . .
>
> Since then—'tis Centuries—and yet
> Feels shorter than the Day
> I first surmised the Horses' heads
> Were toward Eternity—
> (#712)

Indeed, that someone began to feel ever more like a friend, no longer passive but magically, sacramentally reaching out to her:

> He touched me, so I live to know
> That such a day, permitted so,
> I groped upon his breast—
> It was a boundless place to me
> And silenced, as the awful sea
> Puts minor streams to rest.
>
> And now, I'm different from before,
> As if I breathed superior air—
> Or brushed a Royal Gown—
> My feet, too, that had wandered so—
> My Gypsy face—transfigured now—
> To tenderer Renown—
> (#506)

Jesus knew the desert Emily knew. Being fully human, he too was shaken by the frequent coldness of the world around him. He wept in Gethsemane and sweated blood. His cry from the cross has resounded down through the centuries. But ultimately he had the will to resist all satanic seductions to despair, because he, like Emily, had the wisdom to savor every utterance, every signal, every clue that comes from God. As a result he too, like Emily, experienced a transfiguration that we will read about in next week's gospel.

SECOND SUNDAY OF LENT

Luke 9:28–36, Mark Twain, Willa Cather

Lent: A Time to Get Real

The word *person* derives from those masks worn by actors in classical times. In Latin such a mask was called a "persona," something through which the actor spoke his lines, which is what actors do even today: lay aside their real identity to take on a temporary personality while on stage. In fact, the word *personality* has been taken over by press agents, so that it's common nowadays to call show biz people "personalities." And often they become so identified with their stage persona, it's hard for them to shake it. For example, Sean Connery will always be James Bond to me.

In this age of the visual media, not only stage folk present a persona, or false face, to the public. Newscasters, sports figures, pundits, all seem to have become pitch men, requiring a staff of make up artists to enhance their image. Witness the disappearance of the line between the stage and even politics in elections like that of a wrestler or actor to high office. Why even we ordinary folk rarely leave the privacy of our homes without adopting a persona, a mask, to wear at work or at the supermarket or even in church.

Yet strangely enough, we also use the terms person or personal or personality to mean the very opposite of a theatrical persona or personality. We use them to refer to one's authentic self. For example, when we are treated with genuine care and intimacy by a bureaucrat at the Department of Motor Vehicles, we come home to say, "He was a real person and he treated me like a person." In other words, we reserve the word person to describe someone who hides behind no mask, who recognizes relationship to be something deeper than merely contractual or legal or "sociable."

The parables of Jesus are full of such "persons," like the Good Samaritan or the forgiving father of the prodigal son. Indeed, parables or stories give us a better sense of personhood in its deeper sense than any abstract definition. Take, for example, Mrs. Loftus in whose home Huckleberry Finn takes refuge disguised as a girl named Sarah Williams (and later Mary Williams!). Mrs. Loftus goes along with it gently until at last she says, "What's your real name? . . . I ain't going to hurt you, and I ain't going to tell on you, nuther. You just tell me your secret and trust me. I'll keep it and what's more I'll help you. . . . Why, I spotted you for a boy when you was threading the needle; now you just trot along to your uncle . . . and if you get into trouble, you send word to Mrs. Judith Loftus, *which is me* [author's emphasis], and I'll do what I can to get you out of it." [12] Now there's a person, a truly personal being who wears no mask and, like God, is not taken in by masks.

Or consider that immigrant woman of Nebraska in Willa Cather's story *My Ántonia* [13] where the narrator says of her: "Ántonia had always been one to leave images in the mind that did not fade— that grew stronger with time . . . Ántonia kicking her bare legs against the sides of my pony . . . Ántonia in her black shawl and fur cap, as she stood by her father's grave in the snowstorm; Ántonia coming in with her work-team along the evening sky-line. She lent herself to immemorial human attitudes which we recognize by instinct as universal and true. . . . She was a battered woman now, not a lovely girl; but she still had that something which fires the imagination, could still stop one's breath for a moment by a look or gesture that somehow revealed the meaning of common things. . . . All the strong things of her heart came out in her body, that had been so tireless in serving generous emotions. It was no wonder that her sons stood tall and straight."

The gospel is all about our similar transfiguration, about resurrecting that potentially Christic personality we all hide under the persona we present to the everyday world. Isn't it time for us to get real?

THIRD SUNDAY OF LENT

Luke 13:1–9

Titanic

In today's gospel the disciples ask Jesus what he thought about recent headlines in the local newspapers. One headline read, "Pilate Ambushes Rebel Galileans. Scores Killed." The other read, "Siloam Tower Collapses. 18 Killed, Many Hurt." The disciples wanted to know whether such disasters were God's way of punishing the victims for their sins. Jesus replies, "Of course not! Disaster victims are no guiltier than anyone else. If accidents were God's way of punishing people for their sins, we'd all be carried off in ambulances."

But just prior to their asking him about this Jesus had been talking about "signs of the times." He said, in effect, "You all know how to read the weather. If you see a cloud in the west, you expect a shower. If you feel a south wind, you expect a heat wave. And yet when it comes to current human events, you're all as blind as a bat. Take these two headlines about a massacre and an accident. Could it be that those disasters are a forecast of what will soon happen on a wider scale if society doesn't wake up and change its attitude?"

All this makes me think about the *Titanic.* What a powerful grip that disaster has upon the world's imagination. Even though it lies at the bottom of the sea, we can't resist going down in submersibles to ponder it, photograph it, and scoop up relics to display (the way a psychologist would have us probe the depths of our unconscious mind to recall events that still affect the way we live). We interview survivors and keep count of them. We replay the event over and over on film and TV. Indeed, isn't it interesting that at the close of the twentieth century a film production of this tragedy that began the century became one of the biggest box office hits in history? It's almost as though we've made the *Titanic* the signature event of our era.

Think of it. On its maiden voyage in 1912, the *Titanic* was the embodiment of the twentieth century at that time. There was an upper class of emperors throughout Europe; aristocracies that could trace their titles back a thousand years. Many of these monarchs didn't have to answer to anybody. And then there was that new aristocracy, the robber barons, people without titles but with immense wealth. Then there were the steerage passengers, the millions of poor worldwide who were at the mercy of the few aristocrats on the bridge. As with the *Titanic,* this century was launched with great optimism, even arrogance. Progress was unsinkable. Science and technology were advancing rapidly, subduing nature to our beck and call. Most of the world, great cultures like India and Islam, was subject to one or another European empire. The next hundred years were bound to be a pleasant cruise.

If it weren't for the unexpected, the unbelievable: World War I, World War II, the Cold War, disaster, technological violence on a scale never witnessed before in history! Now all those monarchies are gone; all those empires have been washed away. If the world's leaders (Jesus might say) had read the lesson of the *Titanic* as clearly as science was able to read the weather, perhaps history might have turned out differently; perhaps a lot of people might have lived who died horrible and premature deaths.

It's too late now, of course, to fix the twentieth century but the lesson of the *Titanic* still has application. At the very least, in keeping with the admonition of Jesus, we ought to be better prepared to interpret early the meaning of any disaster that marks the beginning of the twenty-first century!

FOURTH SUNDAY OF LENT

Luke 15:1–32

The Prodigal Father

Ask for a reservation for brunch anywhere on Mother's Day and you'll hear, "Sorry, we're all booked up." But on Father's Day? Take your pick! Fatherhood doesn't have the marketability of mother-hood in our culture—probably because it's too often equated with patriarchy and all its connotations of authority, law, discipline, and the prospect of a session behind the woodshed.

I looked upon my father with some ambivalence. Would he be daddy today or the dour adjudicator of my case? And, of course, the homestead is but a microcosm of our larger political and other institutions, where patriarchal figures (often endowed with false *gravitas*) have traditionally served as society's legislators and enforcers. Indeed, this juridical notion of paternity tends to define God himself as our supreme patriarch, the enigmatic arbiter of whether we shall ultimately merit a paternal pat on the head or a clout behind the ear.

The scribes, who used to complain of Jesus' consorting with sinners, came out of such a patriarchal or juridical sense of God. They were therefore prone to evaluate and accuse almost reflexively in his name. And so Jesus decides to confront them with another sense of fatherhood. He tells them the parable of the Prodigal Son.

Now, as Jesus narrates the son's domestic defiance, culminating in his competing with swine for garbage, the scribes think, "So far, so good. Let the punishment fit the crime." Nor are they less impressed by the son's quite orthodox reaction to his predicament: He admits he's done wrong and is ready to pay the price. He even practices a formula of repentance learned under scribal tutelage:

Item # 1: "Father, I have sinned against heaven and you";
Item # 2: "I no longer deserve to be called your son";
Item # 3: "Treat me as your hired servant."

The whole cadence of the story remains compatible with the patriarchal mindset of the audience. But then Jesus pulls a coup de théâtre, something that changes the whole direction not only of the story but of the whole universe. Instead of preparing to cross-examine the son, the father rushes to meet and embrace him. Before the son can completely mouth his formula of repentance, the father impedes his speech with kisses. Now the listening scribes are less concerned about the boy than they are about the un-patriarchal behavior of the father! He's totally out of character. He's ad-libbing things like: "Quickly bring the finest robe; put a ring on his finger and sandals on his feet" (Luke 15:22), as he conveys his son off this world's juridical stage into a realm of grace too incomprehensible to describe to scribes.

And yet why should that father's behavior be incomprehensible? As a father I can understand it. True, fathers are not associated with love as much as mothers are, simply because of the patriarchal burden imposed on them in this fallen world. But I can testify there is such a thing as fatherly love—a love perhaps not always so vocal because its quintessential characteristic is one of awe, wonder, amazement, perpetual fascination over his son or daughter; something likely to leave him speechless except for the embarrassing tears in his eyes.

In this parable Jesus says that if we must describe God as a father, then he's that kind of father, a God who simply adores us (even as I adore my sons), a God who is in a constant state of wonder over each and every one of us and longs only to embrace us and thereby recharge our own hearts with a love as powerful as his—powerful enough to change the world.

FIFTH SUNDAY OF LENT

John 8:1–11

Jesus Bent Down and Began to Write . . .

My younger son Philip, in the year before he died, felt a need to have a business card made up such as professionals use to identify themselves and their credentials. He presented one to me at one of our now so memorable breakfasts in San Francisco (at Hamburger Heaven on Clement Street and sometimes at Bill's Place farther out). The card simply said

> Philip B. Wood
>
> Failure
>
> 415-864-1196

I didn't know whether to laugh or cry. Actually I laughed because Phil and I shared the same perverse sense of humor, and I guess by then we had both come to agree that Phil was not going to make it according to the prevailing standards of this world. I thanked him for the card and before slipping it into my wallet inscribed in pencil on the back his current address. He passed away not long after that and over the years, as the address has begun to fade, I take out a pencil and re-inscribe it to keep it fresh—I guess out of some wish to keep him and our moments together alive. And it works.

This brings me to my other son, Adam, who, while maintaining a wonderful integrity, has never had difficulty fitting into this workaday world. Indeed, convinced early on of the dignity of labor, he took pride in having had a sheet metal worker for a grandfather and one day, having noticed his grandfather's portable toolbox in my garage, asked if he could have it. The box had a wide patch of white bandage tape under the handle on which my father had inscribed his name and address in ink. Some years later, while visiting Adam, I came upon the toolbox again and much to my surprise the once almost illegible name and address on the tape now stood out more sharply than I remembered. Why? Because Adam periodically takes out a pen to restore the aging letters one by one. And I'm sure that somewhere beyond the wide blue yonder, my father remains deeply moved by this gesture of a grandson he never lived to see.

Do you know what a palimpsest is? The word comes from the Greek, meaning "erased again." It derives from a time when copyists, given the shortage of writing materials, would often erase the original writing on a manuscript to acquire space to pen an entirely different text, with the result that traces of the original writing peek faintly from beneath the letters of the fresh writing. Such manuscripts are called palimpsests. For example, in Paris we have a thirteenth-century palimpsest of the essays of Saint Ephraem beneath whose letters traces of an erased fifth-century Greek Bible are still legible.

All of this makes me think: Are not you and I palimpsests? Are we not each a manuscript on which over the course of our lives one script after another has been imposed, the latest script overlaying all prior scripts? Initially our once-fresh manuscript contained only a baptismal statement declaring you and me to be each another Christ born into this world. Thank God that original script was indelible, because how many times have we tried to erase it, to bury it deep beneath one fashionable ideology or identity after another? Yet that barely visible, barely legible story of who and what we really are pokes its way from beneath the mishmash and scribbling we have made of our lives—waiting for Christ to return at every eucharist we attend to refurbish that fundamental text within us, that good news you and I are meant to be—much the way I refurbish my Philip's precious address and Adam, his grandfather's immortal name.

PALM SUNDAY OF THE LORD'S PASSION
GOSPEL AT THE PROCESSION

Luke 19:28–40, Charles Dickens

Two Kinds of Revolution

There is no doubt many in the crowd that cheered Jesus' arrival in Jerusalem were hoping he would start a revolution. They hoped he would overthrow the Romans and all who profited from Roman imperialism at the expense of the disenfranchised. They were, of course, to be sadly disappointed. Jesus did, indeed, come to promote a revolution, but not the political kind that has become somewhat commonplace throughout the world over the past two centuries.

Charles Dickens gives us a pretty good study of this type of revolution in his novel *A Tale of Two Cities*.[14] You always have two opposing parties. You have those at the top, like the French aristocrats, who have and hold fast to everything, for whom: "It was the best of times . . . the season of Light . . . the spring of hope," and those at the bottom who had nothing, for whom "it was the worst of times . . . the season of Darkness . . . the winter of despair." And then the wheel turns. The bottom rises; the top comes crashing down like the blade of the guillotine. And then what? The oppressed become the oppressors to be overthrown by the next generation of have-nots. "Sow the same seed of rapacious license and oppression over again," says Dickens, "and it will surely yield the same fruit according to its kind."

But I think, while vividly describing your ordinary political revolution, Dickens also gives us a glimpse of the kind of revolution or revolutionary Jesus came to promote. Among the many terrified or raging characters of the novel, two stand out as agents of Christ. There's Mr. Lorry, a 70-year-old employee of a British bank, who in the process of managing the affairs of his clients, insures the survival of the infant daughter of a man imprisoned in the Bastille, later reunites that prisoner with his now grown daughter, and helps in the rescue of that daughter's husband from the bite of the guillotine. And all the while he downplays his generosity by insisting he's simply being a businessman attending to his business! No feelings involved, if you please. Just conducting business.

And then there's Sidney Carton, a dissolute lawyer, cynical about life and politics until the words read at his father's grave ("I am the Resurrection and the Life: he that believeth in me, though he were dead, yet shall he live: and whosoever liveth and believeth in me shall never die") infiltrate his consciousness, revive his faith and heart to the point where he goes to the guillotine himself that others may live and find happiness.

How do these Christic revolutionaries differ from the top dog and the underdog of your ordinary revolution? Well, whereas the latter are characterized by "I have and will hold fast" and "I want and will take," ultimately issuing in violence, Mr. Lorry and Sidney Carton are "givers"; they hold fast to nothing, they intervene, they put themselves at risk for others, they do not grab, they embrace, they are all heart—in the manner of Christ. And until we all become like that, the ultimate revolution, that quantum leap in human relations we all wish for, will be delayed.

Still, Christ's revolution remains ever at work undermining the philosophy of greed that marks our world, granted its true emissaries are sometimes not easily noticeable. Why, my goodness, one of them might even be that bank employee you saw coming out of Rotary the other day, or one of them might be one of those lawyers we're always insulting (who does so much pro bono work nobody's aware of).

PASSIONTIDE

Passion Narratives

Passion Play

While watching the Passion Play put on by our parish on Palm Sunday, and especially while listening to the loud hammer blows as the players nailed Jesus to the cross, I couldn't help but think how morbid all this might seem to some visiting nonbeliever. "What are these people doing?" he might think. "These Christians are surely sadomasochists to make a man's execution the central feature of their religion—to display constantly before their congregations the image of a man suspended on a cross, crowned with thorns, blood flowing from his hands, feet and side. How gloomy can you get! Why don't they contemplate something more sublime and wholesome like springtime and fertility, life instead of death?"

I'm glad I let that rebellious thought cross my mind, because it forced me to justify and appreciate our focus on the crucifixion of Jesus.

Christianity refuses to be an escapist kind of religion, a provider of pleasant fantasies that distract from what we are. Christianity displays before our eyes the death of a Poet, and not only that—it reveals our involvement in that death. It is we who say this Poet is expendable, a nuisance. It is we who cry out, "Crucify the Poet!" It is we who prefer the "tough guy," Barabbas, to the Poet, Jesus. It is we who, even if we feel a passing compassion for the Poet, tolerate (like Pilate and Peter) his destruction.

Christianity tells us loudly and clearly what's wrong with us as individuals and a society. We kill poets. We kill people who envision and insist upon a world of mutual forgiveness and therefore Beauty. We are embarrassed by human beings like the poet Shelley who sense how

> The awful shadow of some unseen Power
> Floats, though unseen, among us; visiting
> This various world with as inconstant wing
> As summer winds that creep from flower to flower[15]

—who call this Power: Beauty, God, Father, the Holy Spirit, and dedicate their own powers to its service.

In repudiating those visionaries, who for us are all summed up in Christ, we repudiate the very Creator of the universe—the original Poet who articulates this marvelous world we live in—and even ourselves as potential poets, purveyors of beautiful deeds. Week in and week out, Christianity confronts us with the consequences of such perversity by displaying above our altars the crucifixion of that Poet whose death is repeated over and over again in the assassination of a Martin Luther King, an Archbishop Romero, and in our own "execution" every time we repress an inspiration to be forgiving, caring, extravagantly generous—to behave beautifully.

But Christianity, having made us face up to this self-destructive tendency, then declares in the resurrection of Christ the inevitable victory of the Poet and of the poetic in us. We cannot erase moral beauty altogether. It will return again and again like the California poppies of spring. The Poet within and among us will win out. That is our ultimate creed, for which reason in ancient churches the crucified Christ was often portrayed not hanging lifeless and naked on a cross but robed in splendor, his eyes wide open and arms outstretched in all-embracing love and on his head a golden crown of victory—after all.

EASTER SUNDAY

Luke 24:1–12, Frances Burnett

Their Eyes Were Opened . . .

This is the first spring I've seen in decades. It's one of my retirement benefits. In prior springs my focus was on the taillights of the car in front of me, rarely on the daffodils and lupines that lined the highway. And once I arrived at the office, I sat entranced for eight hours before a computer screen, unresponsive to the seduction of the playful clouds and azure sky outside my window.

Free at last, I'm now able to take a walk every morning (sometimes around the Plaza neighborhood or through one or another of the regional parks) and watch the sun come up like the elevation of some gigantic host to bathe the hills and homes of the valley in gold, to reveal thousands of diamonds glistening upon fields of grass. And I'm able to watch the trees react: the evergreens standing erect and tall, majestic in the light of such majesty; the oaks, willows, maples, and fruit trees reaching out randomly as though caught up in some grateful dance, their movements too deliberate to be seen by human eyes, the music too subtle to be heard by human ears. And then there are the blossoms, pink, white, lavender, yellow, which I thought used to fade too fast, now greeting me day by day for what seems an eternity, rewarding me for my attention and serving as acolytes at this grand liturgy otherwise known as a spring morning.

It's as though, after decades of preoccupation, I have recaptured a glimpse of that Garden of Eden the Bible says we lost ages ago—into which that gardener, the risen Christ, whom the weeping Mary Magdalen met on such a morning, would lead our catechumens and us every year at Easter time.

I am reminded of the boy Colin in Frances Burnett's *The Secret Garden*.[16] He lived an invalid at Misselthwaite Manor. His mother had died at his birth; his father, unable to bear reminders of her, had closed her garden and gone abroad. His only other relative was a cousin named Mary (an orphan) who had recently arrived to live at the manor. It was she who found and reopened the closed garden that spring for the first time in 10 years and with a shepherd boy, Dickon, cultivated it back to its original beauty. She didn't know Colin existed until she heard his crying one day. She found him pale and bedridden and remarked, "What a queer house. Rooms are locked up and the gardens are locked up—and you! Have you been locked up?"

Apparently his father's grief made Colin feel guilty over his mother's death, which translated into physical ailments and a con- viction that he himself was soon to die. Well, Mary and Dickon knew that all Colin needed was exposure to the sacramental wonders of the secret garden. So they took him in his wheelchair to the garden gate, relating to him (like good RCIA sponsors) how they themselves first found the garden, guided by a robin. "And here is the handle and here is the door," said Mary (like a good RCIA instructor). "Dickon, push him in—push him in quickly!" And Colin with a gasp of delight (like a good catechumen) covered his eyes with his hands until they were inside, only then to take them away and look round and round as Dickon and Mary had once done. "Everywhere were splashes of gold and purple and white and . . . fluttering of wings and faint sweet pipes and humming and scents. . . . And the sun fell warm upon his face like a hand with a lovely touch." And Colin stood up and cried out, "I shall get well! And I shall live forever and ever and ever!" I feel like Colin this spring. Or like that Mary who once upon a time, having experienced a similar garden, rushed to tell the disciples, "I have seen the Lord."

SECOND SUNDAY OF EASTER

John 20:19–31, Ernest Hemingway

The Lost Generation

That's how Gertrude Stein described the young American expatriates who led a bohemian life in Paris in the 1920s. Among them was Ernest Hemingway who would write novels that established the skeptical "loner" as the twentieth century's American male role model—the mold out of which the Gable-Bogart-Mitchum-Eastwood dynasty would emerge. Brought up prior to the First World War, Hemingway's generation had been taught to believe in the eventual triumph of reason and progress, and to trust the wisdom of the prevailing political and economic systems and leaders. And then the most destructive war in history exposed the actual stupidity of those leaders, rendering every system and value questionable.

The hero of Hemingway's *A Farewell to Arms*[17] is just such a disillusioned young man. Wounded on the Italian front, Frederic Henry had already atrophied into a neutral observer of life. He listened politely but without commitment to the agnostic, atheist, liberal, or socialist philosophies of his military comrades. To him (as to Hemingway) life might have its occasional pleasures but must ultimately turn out tragically meaningless. But no sentimentality, no whining please! Rather, face the challenge like a matador facing the bull, which will inevitably gore him someday but never deprive him of his poise, his dignity.

Still, Hemingway harbored a spiritual nostalgia of sorts, for he has Frederic meet a young Italian army chaplain who is the daily target of the anticlerical officers' ridicule. He's from the Abruzzi, a remote, mountainous, and behind-the-times province of Italy whose people were pious and poor but hospitable—a region symbolic of the long forgotten Age of Faith. When Frederic earlier in the story goes on leave, the priest suggests he visit the

Abruzzi. But Frederic opts instead for the sensuality of the secular city and upon his return expresses regret: "I had wanted to go to Abruzzi. . . . I had gone to no such place but to the smoke of cafes and nights when the room whirled and you needed to look at the wall to make it stop."

Later, when Frederic is convalescing from his wounds, the priest visits him again bringing gifts and Frederic notices he looks sad. He asks what he will do after the war and the priest's face is suddenly very happy: "If it is possible I will return to the Abruzzi." Frederic asks, "You love the Abruzzi?" "Yes," says the priest, "I love it very much." "You ought to go there then," says Frederic. The priest replies: "I would be too happy. If I could live there and love God and serve Him. There in my country it is understood that a man may love God. It is not a dirty joke." "I understand," says Frederic and then the priest hits home: "You understand but you do not love God. . . . You should love Him. What you tell me about in the nights. That is not love. When you love you wish to do things for. You wish to sacrifice for. You wish to serve." Frederic admits, "I don't love." "You will," says the priest. "Then you will be happy."

I can't help but see in that exchange between the priest and Frederic an episode equivalent to Christ's confrontation with Thomas in today's gospel. Thomas was traumatized by the crucifixion. Frederic, traumatized by the war, was beginning to lock his heart to any notion that life could make sense. And yet by way of this priest from Abruzzi (where, as Hemingway writes, "the spring was the most beautiful in Italy"), Christ comes to Frederic with the same invitation he makes to Thomas: "Be not unbelieving but believe." Thomas, of course, succumbed to the invitation. As for Frederic or Hemingway? Maybe not. Except that it is said that at his death, Hemingway's family requested a priest to preside over his burial.

THIRD SUNDAY OF EASTER

John 21:1–19, Kathy Evans

Freedom

Kathy Evans is a poet who encourages residents of a juvenile justice institution not only to read poetry but to write a poem or two. Now writing poems isn't easy—at least for me—because poetry requires that we speak from the heart, express ourselves personally, soul to soul. It requires that we engage both subjectively and objectively with reality. It requires that we be candid, meaning: aglow, even white-hot. A poem therefore differs from a lecture, because a lecture is generally a collection of abstract statements purged of emotion lest its accuracy be questioned.

Jesus never lectured. He was always personal in his utterances, even in his briefest exchanges. For example, when he was by the Sea of Galilee and met Peter, who was still full of remorse over his threefold denial, Jesus didn't lecture him about treachery and repentance. He simply asked, "Simon, do you love me?" Nor when it came to issues like poverty or grief did he appropriate the parlance of a pedantic sociologist. He spoke rather from the depths and anguish of his heart: "Blessed are you poor, for yours is the kingdom of God. Blessed are you who mourn, for you shall be comforted." Jesus was always personal and therefore everything he says in the gospels is laden with poetic eloquence.

Which brings me back to Kathy Evans's effort to cultivate poetry within the walls of a criminal justice institution—because what could be a less poetic and therefore a less personal environment! And yet how desperately the residents of such an institution are in need of personality, of reviving their capacity to speak from the heart, to engage soul to soul, to reconnect candidly and courageously with the world and the source of the world around them. (Indeed, how desperately we all need to revive that capacity!)

This is what happens, then, so wonderfully in the case of Marcel, to one of Kathy's students, who is the subject of her own poem "Today in Juvy."[18]

> Marcel says
> he's gonna sing his poem,
> that two weeks ago he didn't even know what a poem was,
> that it just came out; . . .
> he says he'd never even written a poem before,
> but this one just wants to be sung,
> and he smiles crooked-like, . . .
> places his arms on the po-di-um in front of him,
> and says, "Now, I know you're gonna want to laugh
> when I sing my poem
> and I'll just ask you brothers
> to wait, to hold your laugh til I'm done,
> I'm just sayin wait."

Kathy goes on to describe his audience of big boys in faded orange shirts with shaved heads, sneering:

> the boys from Richmond, from the turf and the hood,
> some with biceps that seemed bolted on,
> they just stared at Marcel,
> watched him close his eyes like a skinny choir boy,
> fill his lungs and sing.

His poem was about his girl and the baby she had (which came out like a poem); how together they made it and lost it. By the time he finished, what a transfiguration of the whole place from anonymity to personal solidarity as Marcel

> sang until the brothers in the back wanted to sing too. . . .
> I swear the whole class was stunned . . .

the guards by the door, the boys at the back,

the parole officer in blue,

the nurse who dispensed small pale pills in dixie cups,

and the poetry teacher, who was all of a sudden

just one of them, one

with them, one with Marcel

and the brothers up in Juvy

because sometimes a poem

just wants to be sung.

Does Jesus reappear at moments like that? Does he arrive in the person of someone like Marcel? I mean the Easter Jesus who was so radically personal and therefore poetic in every way? I mean the Jesus who began his career reading an old poem of Isaiah about setting captives free?

FOURTH SUNDAY OF EASTER

Revelation 7:9, 14–17, John 10:27–30, Marcel Proust

A Little Patch of Yellow Wall

Bergotte was an old writer admired by Marcel, the hero of Proust's novel *In Search of Lost Time.*[19] In that wandering story, Marcel recalls how Bergotte became very ill and was advised by doctors to rest. Then one day he read a newspaper review of an exhibition of paintings by the seventeenth century artist Vermeer. In the review the critic mentioned a little patch of yellow wall in Vermeer's painting of the Dutch town of Delft, observing that it was a thing of beauty all by itself. Bergotte knew that painting very well and felt embarrassed he had never noticed that detail.

So, ignoring his doctors' advice, he dressed and went to visit the exhibition. Dizziness hit him as he mounted the museum steps, but he managed to make his way to the Vermeer in question. Now, for the first time, his eyes found that tiny patch of yellow wall. He gazed upon it "like a child upon a yellow butterfly that it wants to catch." And then he thought, "That's how I ought to have written. My last books are too dry. I ought to have gone over them with more layers of color, made my language precious in itself, like this little patch of yellow wall."

Now, remember, Bergotte was risking his life to do what he did. It was as though savoring that little patch of yellow wall meant more to him than life itself. And, indeed, no sooner did he sit down on a circular settee before the painting, repeating to himself over and over "Little patch of yellow wall," than he slipped to the floor. Attendants rushed to assist him, but he was dead.

Telling of that incident, Marcel goes on to wonder: Was Bergotte really dead? For that matter, is Vermeer or any artist or saint really dead? Can anyone who, like Christ, can perceive the beauty of this world and unveil it for us, bring out the everlasting worth of every transient thing, be anything but everlasting himself?

Skeptics scoff at any notion that we are immortal. And yet— asks Marcel—whence do we derive this obligation we feel "to do good, to be kind and thoughtful, even to be polite," or for an artist to feel "obliged to begin over again a score of times a piece of work . . . like that patch of yellow wall painted with so much skill and refine-ment"? (Or whence does a Mother Teresa feel obliged to see beauty in the street people of Calcutta and devote her life to them?) Marcel can only assume that all "these obligations . . . seem to belong to a different world, a world based on kindness, scrupulous-ness, self-sacrifice, a world entirely different from this one and which we leave in order to be born on this earth, before perhaps returning there to live once again beneath the sway of those unknown laws which we obeyed because we bore their precepts in our hearts, not knowing whose hand had traced them there— those laws to which every profound work of intellect brings us nearer and which are invisible only—if then!—to fools."

He concludes, then, that Bergotte's immortality was by no means improbable. "They buried him," he writes, "but all through that night of mourning, in the lighted shop windows, his books, arranged three by three, kept vigil like angels with outspread wings and seemed, for him who was no more, the symbol of his resurrection."

Are you polite even when you don't have to be? Do you feel obliged at times to behave beautifully instead of critically or vindictively or carelessly? Are there things or people worth more to you than life itself? According to Marcel, these are symptoms of your own immortality; evidence that you have already learned to hear the creative voice of the Risen Jesus, to imbibe from his everlasting springs; evidence already that you have become an implement within his redemptive grasp.

FIFTH SUNDAY OF EASTER

Revelation 21:1–5, Rainer Maria Rilke

I Saw a New Heaven and a New Earth

When someone you love dies suddenly, the world seems so empty. Work, supper, errands, bills, plans—everything seems so irrelevant. Your mind and heart are elsewhere. The landscape as you drive to work now looks strange—like the receding panorama viewed from the rear platform of a railway coach, like a world taken over by the past tense.

I wouldn't call it simply a state of depression. There is something positive or curious about it. I think you begin to feel distant from your everyday surroundings because the death of the one you love has made you suddenly more conscious of other dimensions you were till then too preoccupied to notice. Caught up in this merely three dimensional world we call the United States of

America or the twenty-first century or "life"; caught up in the daily melodrama of the workplace, in the ever changing, never changing politics of experience; performing the several roles of breadwinner or housewife or entrepreneur or bureaucrat or "life of the party"; reciting the lines expected of us—it's no wonder we assume that this theater of our own preoccupations is the only world there is.

And then someone like my young son suddenly departs and you experience grief yes, but also what the poet Rainer Maria Rilke describes in a poem called "Death Experienced."[20] "The world is full of roles we act," he says

> But when you went, a streak of reality
> broke in upon this stage through that fissure
> where you left: green of real green,
> real sunshine, real forest.
>
> We go on acting. Fearful and reciting
> things difficult to learn and now and then
> raising gestures; but your existence,
> withdrawn from us and taken from our play,
>
> can sometimes come over us, like a knowledge
> of that reality settling in,
> so that for a while we act life
> transported, not thinking of applause.

No, that initial sense of emptiness or distraction we feel when someone we love suddenly departs this life cannot be simply called depression. It can be the commencement of an awareness of a realm so real, so wonderful, so durable that it transforms if only for a little while this three dimensional world into something as precious and transparent as the rose window of some great cathedral.

I am so grateful to a friend for giving me this poem unwittingly on the second anniversary of the very hour I received a call that my son was dead.

SIXTH SUNDAY OF EASTER

John 14:23–29, Robert Service

Whoever Loves Me . . . We Will Come to Him

When I was twelve years old and a mere tenderfoot boy scout, our troop went on a trip to Treasure Island, a scouting reservation situated in the middle of the Delaware River between Pennsylvania and New Jersey. The island lay just a few miles above the place where George Washington crossed the Delaware on Christmas Day in 1776 to surprise the Hessians at Trenton.

It was a similar wintry day when we rowed across to the island to spend a weekend in its big, cold lodge. I remember only two things from that weekend, aside from almost freezing to death. I recall how we pious Catholic boys rose early on Sunday morning, rowed across to the Pennsylvania shore, hiked on empty stomachs to Frenchtown, went to Mass (to avoid committing a mortal sin), hiked back to our boats, rowed back to the island, arriving about noon—only to find all the Protestant boys still in bed and no breakfast made! And they seemed to feel no remorse over this— one more proof of the inferiority of their creed. (We Catholics were quite superior when it came to remorse.)

The second thing I remember is my being taken aside by some older scouts just prior to our departure for home and told to go fetch a bucket of steam. They told me where generally to look and I naively went off, spending about an hour in the snowy woods, and then gave up. When I returned they said, "No matter, we don't need it now; what we need are some skyhooks, which you'll find up along the shore." Off I went again. After about a half hour I came upon a narrow pier and decided to look beneath it.

And there they were, about twelve skyhooks tightly tied to an iron bar. I returned just as the last boat was leaving and said to my mentors, "I found the skyhooks but I couldn't cut them loose." They eyed me curiously and told me to get into the boat.

It wasn't till some time later that they let me in on the joke. And I, too, was amused at how gullible I had been, though I had the satisfaction of leaving them wondering about the skyhooks, which were probably canoe anchors. Later on in life, I thought back to that incident as perhaps part of my initiation into this modern world of ours, where doubt is more fashionable than faith, where we learn not to believe everything we hear. No bucket of steam? Then perhaps no angels, no heaven, no miracles, no God?

But as time went on I came to realize that God (and that hidden dimension of reality that God represents) is not really something we go looking for like some bucket of steam or hidden Easter egg or new continent. God is something we "experience," someone who finds us. God is a "need" we feel when those inevitably difficult, even tragic moments in life strike home. Robert Service says as much in his poem "The Quest."[21] He speaks of searching for God on purple seas, on peaks aflame, amid the gloom of giant trees. "The wasted ways of earth I trod: In vain! In vain! I found not God." He sought him in the hives of men, in cities grand, in temples old beyond his ken. "Alas, I found not God." Until (and I can swear to this!):

> . . . after roamings far and wide,
> In streets and seas and deserts wild,
> I came to stand at last beside
> The death-bed of my . . . child.
> Lo! as I bent beneath the rod
> I raised my eyes . . . and there was God.

THE FEAST OF THE ASCENSION OF THE LORD

Ephesians 1:17–23, Thomas Traherne, John Keats

Dumnesse

In his poem called "Dumnesse,"[22] the seventeenth-century writer Thomas Traherne suggests that Adam in the Garden of Eden was pleasantly ignorant of language. Awed by all he saw around him he remained spellbound, speechless.

> Sure Man was born to Meditat on Things,
> And to Contemplat the Eternal Springs
> Of God and Nature, Glory, Bliss and Pleasure;
> That Life and Love might be his Heav'nly Treasure:
> And therefore Speechless made at first, that he
> Might in himself profoundly Busied be . . .
>
> This, my Dear friends, this was my Blessed Case;
> For nothing spoke to me but the fair Face
> Of Heav'n and Earth, before my self could speak . . .

But the moment Adam began to say, "Wow!" and "Look at that!" and "Look at this!" and began to name and classify things, evaluate them, compare them by judging and "proving" this to be prettier than that and this tree to be more desirable than some other tree—the spell was broken. Tedious chatter usurped his original awe and delight. Having given up silent contemplation for aggressive "talk," he gave up bliss as well—or as Traherne himself put it:

> *I then my Bliss did, when my Silence, break.*

We his descendants have been caught up in similar chatter ever since. We have all been born into a world of adversarial discourse coming at us out the newspapers and TV. We engage in it during coffee breaks and over the dinner table. We have fallen into a world of constant argument over what's mine and what's yours, who's right and who's wrong.

We have created an environment of nonstop litigation in and out of courtrooms. We have in fact turned our world into one grand courtroom where we have all become judges and juries, spouting verdicts, imposing sentences upon each other individually and as ethnic groups or nations or churches. We even tend to view God as a Judge instead of the original Creator/Poet he is. And the consequences of all this polarized discourse? Wariness and war, meanness ranging from petty to horrific. One wonders how we may ever be extricated from the din.

Well it takes some doing! For instance, in the book of Job God has to use a whirlwind to stop Job's chatter. Job was not only articulate but also awfully longwinded when it came to declaring his rights and wrongs. For 30 chapters he petulantly demands that God arrange reality to suit Job's sense of justice and equilibrium. God finally brings the discourse to an end by sweeping him aloft and confronting him with all the immensity and variety of the universe. He shows him the source of the stars, the storehouses of the snow, the mating of mountain goats, until Job is silenced, struck dumb before the wonders of a reality that make his own egocentric concerns seem trivial. In other words, God returns Job or reduces Job to that original, reverent, pregnant silence that characterized Adam before the Fall.

Our tradition would do the same for us during this season of Ascension and Pentecost. It invites us to ascend with Christ above and beyond the din of inherited controversy, to attain a vantage point from which we might quietly contemplate or inhale the prospect of a universe pulsating with grace and mutual forgiveness—even as John Keats described Cortez, when first he gazed with eagle eyes upon the vast Pacific:

> —and all his men
> Looked at each other in wild surmise—
> Silent, upon a peak in Darien.[23]

Silent, yes, but only as prelude to our acquiring a new way of talking, a new way of articulating ourselves as poets, lovers—possessed of fiery tongues that come of God's inspiration, God's Spirit flooding our being.

SEVENTH SUNDAY OF EASTER
FEAST OF THE ASCENSION

Acts 1:3

Forty Equals Fifty

Forty is a number frequently used in scripture. Here are a few examples:

• Noah experiences 40 days and nights of rainfall before the skies clear and a dove returns with evidence of dry land.

• Moses spends 40 days and nights on Mount Sinai prior to descending with the Ten Commandments.

• The Israelites spend 40 years wandering through a desert in search of the Promised Land.

• The prophet Elijah journeys through a desert for 40 days and 40 nights to meet God on Mount Horeb.

• Jesus spends 40 days and nights in a desert preparing for his future ministry.

• The disciples are educated and consoled by the risen Christ for 40 days prior to his ascension.

Why 40 all the time? Like many numbers in the Bible, it has symbolic value. Forty signified the number of years one might expect to live in ancient times. Forty therefore became synonymous with "a lifetime." That being the case, we can understand how the early church might see in all such 40-day or 40-year episodes parables analogous to the span of time we spend in this world. For instance, as with Noah, our life span may seem deluged by worries and frustrations until we've had it up to here! But the Noah story consoles us with the knowledge that someday we, too, will experience an end to this downpour and a rainbow to boot.

Or, like the Israelites in the desert, we, too, seem to spend a lifetime wandering about a barren landscape, wondering if we shall ever find a Promised Land. The Exodus story consoles us with a forecast that we will, indeed, someday finally discover that realm flowing with milk and honey. So also with the 40 days the disciples spent with the risen Christ. For some early church fathers, those 40 days symbolize the time that we, as the church, spend in this world being educated by Christ's word and comforted by his eucharistic presence.

So much for the number 40. But what about the number 50? After all, Pentecost marks the close of the 50-day period after Easter. Did 50 have any significance to those early interpreters of the Bible? You can be sure it did! Fifty was a numerical symbol for the Holy Spirit, that divine force not immediately visible to us in this finite world but as present as, say, the number 50 is within the number 40.

"What's that?" you say. "The number 50 contained within 40?" Well, line up all the numbers by which 40 can be evenly divided. You'll end up with the numbers 20, 10, 8, 5, 4, 2, and 1. And what do they add up to? The number 50! A latent 50 within the smaller 40— even as the boundless Holy Spirit (the power behind the poetry, music and deeds of compassion that make our world beautiful) works imperceptibly within each of us to render us as radiant as the risen Christ himself.

PENTECOST SUNDAY

Acts 2:1–11, Marcel Proust

Just Tap on the Wall If You Need Me

In the Acts of the Apostles, the Spirit descends upon Jesus' disciples with a bang! Lots of special effects such as a loud wind and fire! Considering how depressed the disciples were over the loss of Jesus, perhaps they needed a jolt to propel them out of that upstairs room where they lay hidden and bewildered. And obviously it worked, because suddenly their anxiety gave way to courageous enthusiasm. Instead of spookiness everywhere, they now began to see visions of a world pulsating with Christic potential—a world needing only their surprisingly new eloquence to evoke all its muted beauty.

More often, however, the Spirit prefers less pyrotechnical ways to massage our battered psyches. Take for example the boy Marcel in Proust's novel *In Search of Lost Time*.[24] He lived a sheltered life either in Paris or his ancestral village of Combray during the 1880s. He knew no other environment. And so it was with trepidation that he had to set out one summer with his grandmother to stay at the seaside resort of Balbec.

Every railway stop along the way raised his anxieties until, upon arriving at Balbec after sunset, everything he saw "stabbed [his] homesick heart." The Grand Hotel where they were to stay especially aggravated his depression, what with its monumental staircase and indifferent staff. By then, all he wanted to do was to find seclusion within his hotel room. But once there, he found it impossible to sleep. The furnishings, curtains and high ceiling were all at odds with the nest he knew in Paris. Indeed, he felt so menaced and alien, he wished he could die.

How similar was Marcel's state of mind to that of the disciples in their upstairs room in Jerusalem! But how ripe a moment, too, for the Holy Spirit to pull off a little private Pentecost to comfort and encourage this boy to face his new environment with engagement instead of fear! No pyrotechnics, of course, but an intervention that would be no less sublime. Here's how Marcel remembers it: "Then my grandmother came in, and to the expansion of my constricted heart opened at once an infinity of space." He goes on to say, "I threw myself into the arms of my grandmother and pressed my lips to her face as though I were gaining access to that immense heart which she opened to me." And she gently responded, "And be sure you knock on the wall if you want anything in the night. My bed is just on the on the other side, and the partition is quite thin." Who can miss the eloquence and guarantee of God himself in that simple remark?

It was also the Spirit in the guise of his grandmother who roused Marcel the next morning to show him Balbec at dawn, to transform his fear into fascination before a vision of a sea so vast and the "snowy crests of its emerald waves." It was also she who, as they sat within the hotel's glass enclosed dining room that morning, opened a window to let in a breeze that sent menus, newspapers, hats and veils flying—much to the chagrin of the other guests, but to her own delight as she sat through it all smiling, even "fortified by the celestial draft." Yes, it's thanks to her unspectacular yet inspired interventions that young Marcel became so reconciled to the strange new world around him that his remembrances of that summer at Balbec are among the most beautifully perceptive passages in Proust's entire masterpiece.

So if, when you're in the doldrums and you feel left out because the Holy Spirit has never descended upon you with all the explosiveness of that Pentecost in Jerusalem, think again. More often than not the Spirit will attempt to infiltrate your heart and mind in ways more subtle but no less potent. For example, by way of a grandmother's compassion, a friend's touch, a vermilion sunrise, or a rose.

THE MOST HOLY TRINITY

John 16:12–15, Mark Twain

The Feast of God

When those rascals Bilgewater and the King sold the runaway Jim back into slavery, Tom Sawyer and Huck Finn decided to free him.[25] They knew Jim was locked in a cabin on Silas Phelps's farm. So Tom suggested he and Huck both think up a plan to get him out. Huckleberry recommended they steal the key out of farmer Phelps's britches when he was asleep, open the cabin door and run for it. "Wouldn't that plan work?" asked Huck. Tom said of course it would. The problem was that it was too simple. A good plan had to be more complicated than that! So then Tom laid out his plan and Huck had to admit, "It was worth fifteen of mine for style and would make Jim just as free as mine would, and maybe get us all killed besides." Tom, you see, was what you might call your quintessential thinker. For the job to be done right, it had to be made as complex as possible—and had to include all the detail of documented escapes like that of the Count of Monte Cristo.

So that night they approached the cabin to get the lay of the land. Huck noticed a window high up on the cabin wall with only a board nailed over it. "Here's the ticket," says Huck. "This hole's big enough for Jim to get through, if we wrench off the board." Tom shakes his head and says, "It's . . . as easy as playing hooky. I should *hope* we can find a way that's a little more complicated than that." Ignoring the window, Tom chose to enter the cabin by way of an attached lean-to. The shed was full of picks and shovels, but Tom felt protocol required they dig their way into the cabin with penknives. He figured that would take them several months and still fall short of some of the greatest escapes in literature that took years. (Huck worried whether Jim would live that long.)

Tom also needed a saw to saw off the bed leg to which Jim was chained. Huck wondered why they couldn't just lift it and slip the chain off, only to be accused again of having the "infant-schooliest" ways of doing things. Tom actually regretted the cabin wasn't surrounded by a moat, like a castle, and even suggested he and Huck dig one. Though the cabin was only one story high, he felt a rope ladder was in order as well as many other items—and all the while, Tom knew that Jim was already free! He had been emancipated in the late Widow Douglas's will!

Clearly Tom was a person so interested in the means that the end became irrelevant. One might wonder whether in adult life he graduated to become a member of the committee that designed the tax code. Give such a person an objective to attain and he'll soon become entranced with the process instead of the product and entangle everyone else in it as well. True, achieving some goals in life (like peace or the reunion of Christendom) may not be easy. But how much of the complexity and inefficiency of human problem solving is traceable to a nit-picking that precludes all play of the human heart and imagination?

Way back in the fourth century, churchmen undertook a major project—to explain as clearly as possible the nature of God. Now that's a much bigger challenge than getting Jim out of a cabin. Understanding God will always be a stretch for the human mind. But when you toss into the process the politics and conflicting philosophies of the theologians involved, it's no wonder it took a century of bitter strife to come up with the conclusion that God is one but also three. There's no denying that the product of their work (the dogma of the Trinity) is a masterpiece of human thought, a work of intellectual architecture that has left saints spellbound. But thank God there was one early churchman around like Huckleberry Finn (namely John, author of those briefest of New Testament letters) who, guided by that Spirit of truth mentioned by Jesus in today's gospel, could see quite simply that "God is Love," and whoever abides in love, abides in God and God in him and her.

THE MOST HOLY BODY AND BLOOD OF CHRIST

Luke 9:11–17, 1 Corinthians 11:23–26

Panis Angelicus

My childhood memories of the feast of the Body and Blood of Christ, or Corpus Christi as it was called then, or perhaps I should say of the Corpus Christi procession that followed the Mass, remain vivid. In Saint Ludwig's parish it stayed within the confines of the church building. All of the parochial school children were involved, processing up and down the aisles in front of the acolytes and the men carrying a golden canopy over the priest, who in splendid robes carried the body of Christ aloft in a silver monstrance. There were flower girls scattering rose petals; there was fragrant smoke spiraling up out of the censers. And, of course, there was music: *Ecce Panis Angelorum* (Lo! the Bread of Angels, food of pilgrims) and *Bone Pastor, panis vere* (O Good Shepherd, bread indeed).

It was only later during my sojourn in a less inhibited Italian parish that I was surprised to see this show burst right out of the church into the alleys and avenues of South Philadelphia to fill the very gutters with rose petals. Remember now that Corpus Christi was celebrated in those days on a Thursday so that all this liturgical pomp and circumstance (candles, incense, acolytes, cloth of gold, children and pious adults with folded hands, music) intruded upon what was a workday with all its workaday traffic!

But because the neighborhood was 99.9 percent Italian, the parade wasn't seen as an intrusion. Customers and dealers along the outdoor market stalls made the sign of the cross as the priest passed by. People in the procession waved or called to neighbors as they stood in their storefronts or looked down from the second story windows of row houses. Of course, the scent of incense had to compete with smell of fish and auto fumes, but otherwise the body of Christ, borne upon this river of faith, dominated those secular streets for a couple of hours before returning to its tabernacle within the portals of a church called King of Peace. (In ancient times, I understand, the priest carrying the host would stop to bless an old tree here, a bridge there, a mill here, a public building there, intent upon magically changing the City of Man into a City of God!)

I'm not sure where such processions take place anymore, what with everyone moving to the widespread, less intimate space of the suburbs and a new theological emphasis on the body of Christ as a sacrament to assimilate and resemble rather than contemplate on a pedestal. But I think the symbolism of those old processions is worth remembering, especially in this secular age when the only parades we see are either commercial spectacles with floats enthroning Miss Bisquik or some Nike celebrity, or military juggernauts where rocket launchers usurp the place of Christ's body and marching boots expel every echo of the *Panis Angelicus.*

But maybe I'm premature in assuming that such Corpus Christi processions have disappeared, because doesn't such a procession commence after every Sunday Mass we attend? Having fed upon the body and blood, soul and divinity of Christ at communion time, don't we all still flow forth from our sanctuaries every week to inundate our neighborhoods, workplaces and schools with Christ's presence in our hearts—to make an otherwise secular world sacred again? Aren't we all collectively the body of Christ made mobile well beyond the confines of his tabernacle? Why then not make it a custom to take a handful of rose petals every morning to scatter furtively here and there at work, school and marketplace as befits our grand procession through this world—to awaken people to the fact that life is not some long day's journey into night but a pilgrimage whose destination is everlasting joy?

SECOND SUNDAY IN ORDINARY TIME

John 2:1–11

The Whole Gospel in One Episode!

During our family's Christmas get-together, the usual gifts were exchanged: pajamas and a sweater for me, necklaces for my mother-in-law, and books, books, books for everybody. But the gift that woke everyone up was a magic kit that I presented to my 32-year-old son. Maybe I was just trying to recapture the flavor of a past Christmas when he was but seven years old and all of his gifts were fun packages like that, but I couldn't resist buying the thing if only to enliven an otherwise predictable ritual. The box (picturing the bits of equipment it contained to perform no less than 10 magical tricks) was passed from person to person amid "oohs" and "aahs"— so much so that I had to reveal the store where I bought it. Indeed, I may now go back there myself to buy another for my personal amusement.

All of this proves that magic still fascinates us modern folk— as do the miracles in the gospels like the one narrated today in which Jesus changes water into wine. "How could he do that?" we all ask. And others say, "Oh, he couldn't possibly do that. It must have some rational explanation." And then people speculate: "He must have sent out to the local liquor store for that forty dollar a bottle vintage," and so on. No doubt the same kind of discussion goes on about Christ's walking on water and curing the deaf and blind and raising Lazarus from the dead—all of which proves again that it's the magical or miraculous that immediately engages us— only to distract us from the full significance of such stories.

Actually the author of today's Cana account would have us focus less on the transmutation of water into wine and more on the meaning of that transmutation. That's why he calls the whole

episode a "sign"—because it has significance! And what is its significance? What is it the story in its deepest sense is trying to say?

Well, according to the early church fathers (who had a
knack for seeing the deeper sense of scripture), the mother of Jesus
in the account is a reflection of Mother Israel or Mother Church,
out of whose womb Jesus was born of the Holy Spirit. And Mother
Israel or Mother Church is concerned that here is fallen humanity
trying ever so hard to make of life something as joyous as a wedding
feast and the party's gone flat. We're out of wine! We've become
so politically polarized, so fragmented by religious controversy, so
given to imbibing insipid philosophies and fads that as a race we're
exhausted, bored. And then Jesus, alive with God's breath, alive with
inspiration, appears among us and Mother Israel or Mother Church
or Mother Mary says, "They have no wine! They have no spirit!
They have no joy, no hope, no vision!" And though Jesus himself
may say, "The timing's not right," that maternal instinct insists that
he act and not delay.

And sure enough, Christ acts. He speaks, he proclaims
a gospel capable of changing our flavorless experience of life into
something alive, sparkling, stimulating—into something similar
to blood red wine instead of the insipid, colorless stuff we've been
swallowing. That's what the story tells us: Christ has come to
revitalize human intercourse, to bring life to a party that's gone
stale, to change us magically from hopeless folk into vital, caring,
magical beings.

And, as a postscript, the church has arranged that the marriage feast of Cana be perpetuated among us by way of the eucharists
we attend so that we ourselves, even in our generation, may taste
and testify that God has indeed kept the good wine until now.

THIRD SUNDAY IN ORDINARY TIME

Luke 1:1–4; 4:14–21, Mark Twain

Why Must Recognition Be So Often—Posthumous?

Tom Sawyer, Huck Finn, and Joe Harper were among those rare people fortunate enough to be present at their own funeral and observe how sadly they were missed. You remember the incident. Tom and his two friends, feeling unappreciated, had run away to a Mississippi island near their hometown. There they could inflate their wounded egos by pretending to be Tom, the Black Avenger of the Spanish Main, or Huck, the Red Handed. Then one day they saw boats dragging the river and realized the townsfolk thought they had drowned. So Tom slipped back into town that night to hear Aunt Polly lamenting, "He warn't *bad,* so to say—only *mischeevous* . . . He never meant any harm, and he was the best hearted boy that ever was . . ." And she began to cry while Mrs. Harper agreed, "Only last Saturday my Joe busted a firecracker right under my nose and I knocked him sprawling. . . . oh, if it was to do over again I'd hug him and bless him for it."[26]

Well, Tom at once returned to the island to gather up Huck and Joe and hide with them next day in the choir loft while the minister deliciously eulogized them before the whole congregation. Then "there was a rustle in the gallery, which no one noticed; a moment later the church door creaked; the minister raised his streaming eyes above his handkerchief, and stood transfixed!" as the three delinquents marched down the aisle. Delinquents? By no means! They were now the treasured darlings of St. Petersburg.

This goes to show we shouldn't jump to conclusions about other people. It happens so often. We settle on one or two characteristics of a person and then figure that's all he is. We turn him into a type. He's either "happy go lucky" (which I assume means he's never sad) or we sum him up as a liberal or conservative (whatever that means). In any case, we write the person off one way or the other, the way St. Petersburg once thought Tom a scamp and Huck the local pariah.

There's nothing smart about such simplistic evaluations of people. Actually it's a sign of mental sloth. We don't want to know too much about the other chap; it requires too much work, time, and sympathy. So we take the easy way and pigeonhole the person as funny or too serious or a crank or pushy or—and here I could list a lot of racial, ethnic and gender epithets that I'd be ashamed to utter.

In the gospel reading begun today and continued into next week, we'll witness the town of Nazareth's shallow evaluation of one of its native sons, Jesus, who dared by his eloquence to upset their provincial notion that he was nothing but a carpenter's son. How sadly they failed to discern what a reservoir of divine might and grace had grown up in their midst!

But who am I to judge Nazareth! Just this week I was reminded of my own old habit of stereotyping people. When I was a kid I used to collect baseball cards. Now I collect memorial cards of deceased friars I once knew, sent to me regularly by my old religious order. They show photos of guys who were once stereotyped as gullible, pompous, the martinet, the Duke, the Silver Fox, the Zombie. Normally I keep these cards stacked face down on a shelf because they remind me too much of my own mortality.

But the other day our biweekly housekeeper found them and decided to stand them all up along the shelf so that now their familiar faces stare right at me: Cyril, Bill, Jerry, Cuthbert, Danny. And the more I look at them, the more they seem to transcend the tags we gave them. Through eternity's filter they now appear to me as personalities who would not have been so unique, had it not been for their peculiarities. And I find myself missing them and loving them and feeling ever so grateful to our housekeeper for resurrecting them.

FOURTH SUNDAY IN ORDINARY TIME

Jeremiah 1:4–5; 17–19, Walt Whitman

Then the Lord Extended His Hand and Touched My Mouth

All great prophets in the Bible have what we call an inaugural vision—that initial experience whereby they know their lives must change. Jacob had a fabulous dream, Moses was confronted by a blazing tree, Isaiah was approached by a fiery angel who touched his lips with a red hot coal and said, in effect: "Go now and by way of your poetry endow my people with your vision. Compel them to see more than their doubts will allow." In the unabridged version of today's first reading it is Jeremiah whose lips are touched by God.

Walt Whitman's initial experience, the thing that turned him into a poet and a prophet, was not so dramatic. In his poem "Out of the Cradle Endlessly Rocking,"[27] he says that what fascinated him when as a boy he wandered along the then desolate beaches of Long Island was a pair of mockingbirds nesting in the month of May:

> Two feather'd guests from Alabama, two together,
> And their nest, and four light-green eggs spotted with brown,
> And every day the he-bird to and fro near at hand,
> And every day the she-bird crouch'd on her nest . . .

And then there's a sad moment:

> May-be kill'd, unknown to her mate,
> One forenoon the she-bird crouch'd not on the nest,
> Nor return'd that afternoon, nor the next,
> Nor ever appear'd again.

What now entranced Whitman was the behavior of the solitary he-bird who for the whole summer, night and day, seemed to keep looking for his mate, calling to her. And Whitman kept vigil, too, blending himself with the shadows. He listened long and thought he understood the song of the mockingbird. It seemed to say

> *O night! do I not see my love fluttering out among the*
> *breakers? . . .*

> *Loud! loud! loud!*
> *Loud I call to you, my love! . . .*

> *Low-hanging moon!*
> *What is that dusky spot in your brown yellow?*
> *O it is the shape, the shape of my mate! . . .*

> *Land! land! O land! . . .*
> *. . . I am almost sure I see her dimly whichever way I look.*

How many of us know that feeling of absolute departure, the loss of someone dear. Beyond a certain day, beyond a certain hour of the day, beyond an entry in a diary dated April 27: blank pages. No entry evermore. And stoics will say to us, "It's all a matter of biology, you know! Don't get too emotional over it or cling to the illusion that your loss is anything but final." And yet, like the mockingbird, we persist in taking up our perch on a post by the edge of that night sea we call Death and sing, call out! Despite the cautions of skeptics, we mockingbirds and human beings persist in this intense desire, this conviction we have that life will somehow survive death, both in and beyond this universe.

Whitman found the mockingbird's song contagious. (Maybe it was the Holy Spirit, who likes to appear as a bird.) He wept. He knew the bird sang also for him and from that moment he says he knew what he was for.

Returning as a man to that place of his inaugural vision, his inspiration to become a poet, a prophet, he addresses that mockingbird of his long ago youth:

> O you singer solitary, singing by yourself, projecting me,
> O solitary me listening, never more shall I cease
>   perpetuating you,
> Never more shall I escape, never more the reverberations,
> Never more the cries of unsatisfied love be absent from me,
> Never again leave me to the peaceful child I was before what
>   there in the night,
> By the sea under the yellow and sagging moon,
> The messenger there arous'd, the fire, the sweet hell within,
> The unknown want, the destiny of me.

I think at that moment Whitman became what Jesus is, what every true prophet, every poet, every true disciple of Jesus is meant to be: a "chanter of pains and joys, uniter of here and hereafter."

FOURTH SUNDAY IN ORDINARY TIME
OPTION

1 Corinthians 12:31—13:13, Michael Chabon

The Ultimate Picklock

While an adolescent in pre-1939 Prague, Josef Kavalier became a disciple of an illusionist named Bernard Kornblum. In the tradition of Harry Houdini, Kornblum specialized in escape acts, working his way out of straitjackets, handcuffs and even submerged post office bags. Naturally, he knew everything there was to know about door locks, padlocks, and combination locks, and he introduced Josef to them and to the tools of his trade such as the torque wrench and pick. And he would say, "The pins have voices. . . . The pick is a tiny telephone wire. The tips of your fingers have ears." Kornblum then put Josef through many tests until he became a good escape artist. But by then Hitler's armies had invaded Czechoslovakia and escape became a matter of necessity instead of entertainment. So Joseph made his way through Siberia to Brooklyn, New York, where he moved in with his American cousin, Sammy Clay. All of this is narrated, of course, in Michael Chabon's recent novel, *The Amazing Adventures of Kavalier and Clay.*[28]

Josef was trained in art as well as stunts and so his cousin engaged him to create a new comic book character. Comic books with heroes like Superman and Captain Marvel were just beginning to catch on and Sammy saw a chance to cash in on the trend. But what would they call their superhero? They brainstormed all night and finally came up—not surprisingly—with "The Escapist," a fellow whom criminals and even Hitler might cage, bury, and submerge but who would always escape to bring them to justice. Working on such a project not only provided Josef with a healthy income, it allowed him to fantasize the eventual escape of his relatives in Europe and encourage American youth to detest Hitler and deliver Europe from its chains. However, on hearing in 1943 of the death of his family in a concentration camp, Josef lost interest in "The Escapist" and comic books. He dropped out of sight, leaving a pregnant Rosa Saks in Sammy's care.

He then found himself trapped within the tightest confinement of all: depression, despair, a sense of futility. Nor could he pick the lock until one day he accidentally came upon Rosa Saks's now 12-year-old son—his son—and the spell was broken. And immediately he recalled a remark of Bernard Kornblum in relation to a story about Houdini.

In 1906 Houdini had accepted a public challenge to free himself from a pair of handcuffs made in the 1760s by Joseph Bramah. No one had ever been able to pick these manacles. And so, on a stage before five thousand people Houdini was cuffed and placed into a black cabinet. The orchestra played, people waited fifteen minutes, twenty more minutes. Houdini emerged sweating and asked for a towel. He reentered the cabinet. An hour went by and finally Houdini's wife asked if she might give her husband a drink of water. This was permitted. Harry drank the water and five minutes later he emerged from the cabinet holding the loosened handcuffs high over his head! Nobody realized that Houdini's wife had put the key into the glass of water—for there was no other way out. Or, as Kornblum concluded, "Only love could pick a nested pair of steel Bramah locks."

Gil Bailie, author of *Violence Unveiled,* has often said that our secular culture still feeds off the capital of Christianity. It may be reluctant to acknowledge the Bible, but it still echoes biblical sentiments. Chabon's novel is an example of that, for where did he get his notion that only love can release us from the fetters that bind us if not from our creed's ancient insistence: "There is nothing love cannot face; there is no limit to its faith, its hope, and its endurance" (1 Corinthians 13:7)? And, I might add, to its cleverness!

FIFTH SUNDAY IN ORDINARY TIME

Luke 5:1–11, John O'Hara

Bread Alone?

Mr. Hart's life was not an easy one. He was a hard worker but his job as car-washer at a garage in New York didn't pay much. Nor did the job's long hours allow him any time to cultivate his relationship with his thirteen year old son, Booker, an introverted lad to begin with. In general, he didn't seem to be getting anywhere and, being Black in the 1940s, he saw little chance of his lot changing.

As if this frustration weren't enough, he also felt guilty, because once a week, unbeknownst to his wife, he played the baseball pool at work. It only cost a dime one day a week, which he took out of his carfare allowance by hitching a ride that day. But it bothered him to indulge himself even that much while his wife tried to make ends meet.

But surprise! One day the bookie came into the garage and said, "Well, Willie, you win the sawbuck," and counted out 10 dollars. Was Mr. Hart elated? No. A lifetime of drudgery had made him too much a worrier to be elated. Indeed, he was troubled. "That money belonged in the sugar bowl. A lot could come out of that money: a steak, stockings, a lot of stuff." But then he'd have to reveal he'd been gambling every week. And besides, here was a chance to buy a ticket to a Yankee game for the first time in twenty years. The temptation was too great. By the time he reached home he had two tickets in hand, one for himself and one for his son. He told his wife a friend gave them to him. So he announced, "Tomorrow me and Booker's going over to see the New York Yankees play."[29]

Did he enjoy the game the next day? Well, up to the fifth inning he did. Then remorse hit him—over his having lied to his wife, over his self-indulgence, and especially over Booker's passive reaction to the game. Obviously the kid was bored, not interested.

"Mr. Hart wished the game was over. DiMaggio came to bat. Ball one. Strike one, called. Ball two . . . it was the crack of the bat that made Mr. Hart realize that DiMaggio had taken a poke at one and the ball was in the air, high in the air." It dropped right into his section. People grabbed, scrambled, and shoved trying to get the ball. Booker sat "hunched up, holding his arms to protect his head and face." Men and kids shouted, "Where's the ball?" But it was gone and for the rest of the game the fans mumbled mystified.

When the game ended, Mr. Hart let the seats empty, then sat with his chin on his fist. "Hey, Pop," said Booker. "Present for you." From inside his shirt he brought out the ball. "Go ahead, take it. It's a present for you," said Booker. Mr. Hart looked down: "I'll be . . . You got it? The ball?" He laughed and slapped his knees: "I'll be damn—boy, some Booker!" He hugged the kid: "You givin' it to me? Some Booker!"

John O'Hara entitled this story "Bread Alone" because he apparently agreed with Jesus that it's not by bread alone or the daily grind that we live, but by way of those surprises in life that remind us there's more to it than the daily grind. We live by way of those moments that carry us beyond a world of grabbing and scrambling and shoving into a world where true affection is the norm—a world Willie Hart caught a glimpse of when Booker said, "Hey, Pop . . . Present for you."

Saint Peter has one of those experiences in today's gospel. He, too, was a man used to laboring all night and coming up empty, a man burdened by remorse, resigned to oblivion—until Jesus invited him to put out into the deep and experience a realm of grace and God that almost swamped his boat.

SIXTH SUNDAY IN ORDINARY TIME

Jeremiah 17:5–8, Luke 6:17, 20–26, George Eliot

The Impact of Otherness upon a Lunar Landscape

Fred Vincy was a likeable young man. He came from a comfortable home, his father being a prosperous manufacturer and mayor of the English town of Middlemarch (the fictitious location of George Eliot's novel of that name).[30] But Fred was also irresponsible. He paid little attention to his college studies and had failed several exams. His real interests were horse racing and Mary (a childhood sweetheart, the daughter of the less-well-off family of Caleb Garth). In neither pursuit was he successful, because his gambling left him 160 pounds in debt and Mary refused to marry him so long as he remained aimless.

Regarding his gambling obligation, he could not count on any help from his strict father. So Fred imposed on the kindly Caleb Garth to pledge security for the debt. This won him extra time to pay it off himself, but by the due date all Fred could come up with was 50 pounds—and so he had to shamefully visit the Garth household to remind Caleb of his pledge to provide the balance of 110 pounds.

The Garth family, of course, was not the kind to shirk its obligations. Despite their close-to-zero bank balance, they were able to give up 92 pounds they had set aside for their son's apprentice training and Mary chipped in the other 18 from her meager earnings. As for Fred, he was very apologetic. He claimed he had tried everything to acquire the balance owed; he feared people would have a bad opinion of him; he doubted Mary could ever forgive him. Mary didn't put up with this whining for long. In effect she said, "What does it matter whether I forgive you? Would that make our [now impoverished family situation] any better?"

In this episode, George Eliot wants to show how egocentric Fred was. He's not so much concerned about his impact on the Garth family as he is about his own image, the poor opinion people will have of him. Eliot then goes on to note how so many of us are brought up that way. We're educated to avoid wrongdoing not so much because it may hurt others, but because we'll look bad or be punished or run the risk of "losing my soul" or because it will backfire on us or embarrass our family. It's that kind of narcissistic morality or piety that Jesus essentially opposes in this month's gospel readings.

For example, applying them to myself, it dawns on me that Jesus would liberate me from my incarceration in a universe inhabited by myself alone. And first of all he would entice me simply to notice other people, to take in their features, become aware of them as something other than the supporting cast of my own stellar status.

He would then entice me to become curious about them— to note their particular qualities, to look for traces of the Holy Spirit, to pause and take them in as I might pause on one of my walks to focus (if only for a couple of minutes) on the fragile beauty of this wildflower or that. Finally he would educate me to sense their joy, rejoice in their gifts, feel their pain, and awake to their needs. In other words, he would teach me to identify with others, to care about them and the world around me even as I care about myself.

According to Jesus, only by thus leaving the lunar landscape of my narcissistic self, the lava waste, the salt and empty terrain described by Jeremiah, will I ever come to discover my true self— the me that is merciful even as my heavenly Father is merciful; the me that is therefore finally alive.

SEVENTH SUNDAY IN ORDINARY TIME

1 Samuel 26:2–23, Luke 6:27–38, Victor Hugo

Now What Was He to Do?

Young David was a war hero and poet as well. Saul envied his popularity and decided to kill him. So David fled and became an outlaw. Today's first reading describes an incident during one of Saul's campaigns to catch David. David and his lieutenant Abishai successfully slip into Saul's camp at night and have a golden opportunity to kill their sleeping oppressor. Abishai highly recommends it. But David spares his king.

David's behavior upset Abishai who fully supported, as much as Saul, the norm that has always run our world: an eye for an eye, a tooth for a tooth. In other words, if someone slaps you, slap him back. It's a principle being applied today in the Middle East, the Balkans, Africa, the marketplace and legislatures, as well as in the back streets of Western civilization, despite the fact that it never quite solves anything. All that it does is perpetuate and escalate resentments. Oh, we admit that mercy, understanding, and forgiveness are admirable (and always desirable when we ourselves are the culprit). But deep down we don't trust them to work.

Still, David's act of mercy appeals to us, as do similar acts down through time and story; for example the climactic one described in Victor Hugo's *Les Misérables*.[31] It has to do with Jean Valjean and the sinister police inspector, Javert. Javert was a relentless upholder of the law, totally dedicated to the principle of "Don't get mad; get even." In his mind the world was made up of good and bad, and the bad—as defined by his society—must be caught and contained. Jean Valjean, having once stolen a loaf of bread and escaped from prison, was clearly bad, and Javert, like King Saul, was out to nail him.

But then, during one of France's many revolutions, Javert is captured as a spy by the rebels and condemned to death. Jean Valjean, though not a rebel, is present and requests the honor of shooting Javert. Javert expects no less of this "evil" man. Jean then takes him out of view of the rebel barricades, cuts the cords on his hands and feet and says, "You're free to go." Javert protests, "I find this embarrassing. I'd rather you killed me." Jean Valjean simply says, "Clear out."

Javert leaves stunned. "Something new, a revolution, a disaster, had occurred to him, and he had to think it over. . . . He could see two ways ahead of him, and this appalled him, because hitherto he had never seen more than one straight line. And the paths led in opposite directions. . . . Which was the true one? . . . A benevolent evil-doer, a man who returned good for evil, a man near to the angels—Javert was forced to admit that this monstrosity could exist. . . . He felt himself diminished beside Jean Valjean. But his greatest anguish was the loss of certainty. He had been torn up by the roots. . . . He could no longer live by his lifelong principles; he had entered a strange new world of humanity, mercy, gratitude and justice other than that of the law. He contemplated with horror the rising of a new sun."

Javert is so shaken that later, upon capturing Jean Valjean again, he reciprocates. He lets Jean go—and then, feeling he has betrayed all his former principles and finding the thought of a gracious universe too confusing, he commits suicide.

What he should have done was join a parish—for every Catholic parish is meant ideally to be a laboratory of grace wherein we find opportunities to transcend the "get even" world outside, to experience and practice grace, to cultivate the one revolution of creative compassion that can put to rest all those secular revolutions of history that have turned out to be little more than devastating replays of the same old script: us versus them, or "the good guys" versus "the bad guys."

EIGHTH SUNDAY IN ORDINARY TIME

Luke 6:39–45, e. e. cummings

Lens Adjustment

I went to the optometrist this week for an annual checkup. There was the usual chart on the wall with rows of letters of diminishing size. There again I was given the usual challenge to recite the tiniest line I could read. I chose the second line from the bottom: F C M B S Y. I read it as P O N 3 8 V. Then came the lens adjustment and, much to my delight, the line became clear. Squinting and guessing gave way to clarity, precision, and the relief that comes of being once more visually in touch with my environment. Or was I?

Are glasses all we need to see things clearly? It depends on what you mean by "see." To see surfaces, to see things three dimensionally, to find a fallen teaspoon, to avoid a traffic accident—for all practical purposes, glasses are the remedy. But to see things multidimensionally; to see ". . . a World in a Grain of Sand / And Heaven in a Wildflower";[32] to see, too, the hurt in a smiling face, the loneliness behind every act of pettiness, the terror cringing behind every act of bravado; to see Christ in a piece of bread—to have that kind of vision requires a level of optometric remedy you won't find in the Yellow Pages.

To acquire that kind of insight you have to open your eyes wide and allow some application of Christ's sermon on the mount (which the church has made clinically available to you in Luke's brief version over these recent Sundays). As a matter of fact, somewhere within the whole text of the sermon you'll find Christ, if I may paraphrase here, talking very much like an optometrist: "If your eyes are sound, your whole body shall walk in brightness. If your eyes are bad, things are going to get relatively dark—and once darkness takes over, things can get doubly dark." Of course, those words are already a test of your spiritual vision, because on Christ's lips they mean so much more than they would if you were to see them merely framed on an optometrist's waiting room wall.

This is what they mean in their deeper sense: If your eyes are influenced by a meanness rooted in your soul, if they are jaundiced by resentment over a slight experienced yesterday or 10 years ago, if they are bloodshot with a crankiness that defies all thought of reconciliation, then you will never see more than such meanness, resentment, and crankiness will allow. Or again, if you let your perception of people and things be narrowed by the biases of ancestors long dead, or of political demagogues or other choreographers of whatever is "in vogue," you might as well grope your way through life than ever expect to stride forth immense of mind and heart amid the immensity of God's world around you.

On the other hand, if you can arrive at that largeness of soul resonant in Christ's sermon on the mount—a largeness that would banish every sneer off your face, that would rather have you postpone all thought of worshipping God until you've been reconciled with your neighbor—a largeness that would make you so obviously candid in all that you do and say that your town's notaries might just as well look for another line of work—a largeness that would have you go the extra mile and never judge but only care about others the way God cares about you—then what radiance! How wide and deep and penetrating your perception of reality will be!

Then will you find yourself replete with gratitude akin to that of e. e. cummings:

> i thank You God for most this amazing
> day: for the leaping greenly spirits of trees
> and a blue true dream of sky; and for everything
> which is natural which is infinite which is yes . . .

> how should tasting touching hearing seeing
> breathing any—lifted from the no
> of all nothing—human merely being
> doubt unimaginable You?

> (now the ears of my ears are awake and
> now the eyes of my eyes are opened).[33]

NINTH SUNDAY IN ORDINARY TIME

1 Kings 8:41–43, Luke 7:1–10, Willa Cather

To the Foreigner Likewise . . .

"Emil had more friends up here in the French country than down on Norway Creek. . . . The Norwegian and Swedish lads down by Norway Creek were . . . cautious and reserved with Emil because he had been away to college, and were prepared to take him down if he should try to put on airs with them. The French boys liked a bit of swagger, and they were always delighted to hear about anything new: new clothes, new games, new songs, new dances."

In this passage from her novel *O Pioneers*,[34] Willa Cather is indulging in a bit of symbolism. She's not really pro-French and anti-Scandinavian. But for many a writer "French" means warm, bright, and alive while "Norway" means cold and wintry dark. And so in the novel the French Catholic parish of Sainte-Agnes in 1890 Nebraska becomes a metaphor of a visionary, hopeful, human community compared to the more cautious, cooler community located by (Brrr!) Norway Creek.

Sainte-Agnes is peopled by individuals like Emil's young friend Amédée and his wife Angélique. Amédée is forever trying to waken Emil (who is Swedish by the way) from his frequent moodiness. For example, he tries to encourage Emil to improve his attitude by marrying one of the parish girls. "See . . . there is Séverine . . . and Joséphine, and Hectorine, and Louise!" But Emil remains shy and Amédée pretends to be disgusted: "Bah! . . . I tell all the French girls to keep 'way from you. You gotta rock in there," he says, thumping Emil on the ribs.

"You gotta rock in there!" That's what the parish of Sainte-Agnes (and any spiritually vital parish) wants to proclaim not only to Emil but to the whole modern world, inhabited as it is by people too timid, too sullen, too independent to believe in anything, to fall into profound love. "You gotta rock in there! Loosen up!" It's the same challenge the early church and Peter put to the leaders of Jerusalem in the Acts of the Apostles when Peter demonstrated the power of Christic love by raising a lame man to his feet, who, leaping and praising God, then followed Peter into the Temple through a gate called Beautiful—which, after all, is what our parishes are supposed to be: gateways to a world called Beautiful.

Even the death of young Amédée later in the story never dampens the vitality of Sainte-Agnes. In a life marked by phases of spiritual growth, Amédée has simply graduated to another dimension where he awaits our arrival. And so it's not at all awkward that on the very weekend when the parish of Sainte-Agnes lays Amédée to rest, the choir is rehearsing a Rossini Mass and the women are busy preparing white veils and dresses and trimming the altar to celebrate the Sunday Confirmation of one hundred boys and girls—a whole new generation of faith, love, and poetic being.

I guess the vital spirit of Sainte-Agnes is best manifest in the cavalcade of forty French boys (with Emil taking Amédée's place) who ride out over the prairie to welcome the bishop. "When the word was given to mount, the young men rode at a walk . . . but once out among the wheat fields in the morning sun, their horses and their own youth got the better of them. A wave of zeal and fiery enthusiasm swept over them. They longed for a Jerusalem to deliver. The thud of their galloping hoofs brought many a woman and child to the door of farmhouses as they passed. 'What fine boys!' the bishop said to his priests. 'The church still has her cavalry.'" Or to put it more sublimely: her chivalry, her *ésprit!*

TENTH SUNDAY IN ORDINARY TIME

Luke: 7:11–17

In illo tempore . . .

In the old days, every gospel episode read at the Latin Mass was preceded by the words *"In illo tempore,"* meaning "At that time." For example, "At that time Jesus said to Peter, 'Follow me,'" or "At that time there was a wedding feast at Cana in Galilee," or "At that time Jesus went across the Sea and a large crowd followed him, and . . . he said to Philip, 'Where can we buy enough food for them to eat?'" and so on.

Now we may think those opening words *In illo tempore,* or "At that time," refer us back to the first century in which such gospel episodes occurred historically. But according to the late Dominican scholar Gerald Vann,[35] those opening words have a more mystical quality. They refer not so much to "that time" back then, but to "that time," that eternal present (above and beyond the grip of calendar time) in which the wonder-working Christ now lives and remains available to us, no matter what century we live in.

Indeed (as Gerald Vann goes on to say), when the great Monsignor Ronald Knox published his English translation of the Sunday gospels (as read in the years prior to the Second Vatican Council), he changed that opening phrase *"In illo tempore"* to read not "At that time" but "At *this* time" to stress the immediacy of each gospel's relevance to us. In other words, he wanted to make it clear that the gospel episode issuing from the lips of the deacon or celebrant is not to be received as a mere record or remembrance of a miracle that happened two thousand years ago but as a miracle about to happen right now among us.

Does the gospel reading tell of the widow of Naim and of how Christ stops a funeral procession to raise her dead son to life? The church today is the widow of Naim and we, the congregation, in one way or another are her moribund, if not dead, children whom Christ will touch eucharistically and bring back to life in every sense of the word.

Does the gospel tell of terrified disciples caught in a perfect storm—tossed upon a night sea, their boat capsizing—when out of the darkness Jesus appears walking upon the water, impervious to the storm, saying, "Take courage, it is I, don't be afraid!"? We, the church today, are those disciples, each in our own way tossed about by the wind and waves of change, possessed of a sinking feeling, wondering whether we'll ever find peace, joy, a safe haven. But like the disciples, we, too, (if we have the heart and eyes to see) will behold the unsinkable Christ coming to us eucharistically across the waves, whispering to each of us: "Don't be afraid. It is I. Take me on board and you will experience a great calm."

Does the Sunday gospel tell of a hungry crowd of people out of whose limited resources Jesus produces a banquet that will satisfy them all and then some? We, today, are that crowd of people. We have followed Jesus into this remote place. Though we live in a society of abundance, we're hungry for more than what sports or stocks or even our secular careers can offer. And so Christ will take the limited resources we bring and eucharistically magnify them in such a way that we, too, shall have a taste of that *In illo tempore,* that eternal present, that quality time in which he stands. And that's not all. We shall leave here transformed ourselves (like those five loaves and two fishes) into persons capable of relieving the spiritual hunger of our families and community—and then some!

ELEVENTH SUNDAY IN ORDINARY TIME

Galatians 2:16, 19–21, Flannery O'Connor

Parker's Back

Parker always referred to himself as O. E. Parker. The O. E. were the initials of the names his parents gave him, names he was too shy to admit to because they were biblical. Parker came of a poor Southern family and retained one pleasant memory of his childhood: He had seen a tattooed man at a circus. So impressed was he that by the time he was 16 he had his first tattoo: an eagle perched on a cannon on the back of his hand.

After five years in the navy, he had accumulated tattoos everywhere on his body except his back: serpents and hearts, a tiger and panther on each shoulder, Queen Elizabeth II and Prince Philip on either side of his stomach—all quite colorful. His wife was not impressed. Being a fundamentalist believer, she thought they were sinful. The only one she'd admit she liked was the chicken. "That's an eagle," Parker protested. "What fool would waste their time having a chicken put on themself?"[36]

Getting tattooed was his way of dealing with depression, which was often, considering the humdrum, aimless life he led. Frustrated by his marriage and job, Parker finally thought of having a tattoo done on his back. He wanted something religious to impress his wife. And then one day, while baling hay, his tractor turned over and set a tree on fire. In a panic he yelled, "God above!" as he felt the hot blast of the tree—even as Moses might have done when he came upon that burning tree in the desert. He got up and drove immediately to a tattoo artist. Now he *definitely* wanted something religious on his back. He settled on a Russian icon type of Christ—with those huge eyes. It took two days to do and when he saw the finished image in a mirror, he turned white and shied away.

Dubious now about what he had done, he sought refuge in the local pool hall. His friends quickly sensed that he had a new tattoo and pulled up his shirt to see. Their initial silence was followed by ridicule: "Christ!" . . . "That boy's a real card!" . . . "Maybe he's gone and got religion" . . . "What'd you do it for?" Returning home in the hour before dawn, he felt strange. It was as if those eyes upon his back were staring right through him—still, straight, all demanding. A peace, gentleness, a sense of being "called," permeated his being.

He reached home just as the sun was rising and knocked on the locked door. In response to his wife's angry "Who's there?" he bent down and whispered through the keyhole: "Obadiah Elihue." He felt somehow compelled to reveal his true name as though he were now forevermore to reveal, never conceal, his true self. When she let him in and saw the tattoo, she screamed, "Idolatry," thrashing his back with her broom, raising welts on the face of Christ. Parker staggered out into the yard and when she looked out the door she saw him leaning against the pecan tree in the bright, golden dawn crying like a baby.

What is this parable by Flannery O'Connor trying to say? Maybe it's saying none of us can escape the gaze of Christ, that unique being whose sermon on the mount and vision of reality constantly haunts and challenges us to rise out of our self-indulgent depression and humdrum, petulant, unimaginative ways of living to become the Obadiah Elihues (Servants of the Lord God) we are meant to be.

Christ insists on becoming incarnate in each of us the way he became incarnate upon the back of O. E. Parker. To allow that to happen may win us only ridicule from nonbelievers and even righteous indignation from Christians! But it's the only way to experience a freedom and joy that will have us one day, like Parker, crying like a newborn babe.

TWELFTH SUNDAY IN ORDINARY TIME

Galatians 3:26–29, Nathaniel Hawthorne

Haunted Houses

Clifford and Hepzibah Pyncheon (brother and sister) lived around 1850 in a once stately but now dark and decrepit house with seven gables.[37] They were the latest descendants of a self-proclaimed Puritan aristocrat who, like the biblical Cain, had a poor man executed to acquire the land on which he built his dynasty. The dying victim, however, uttered a curse to insure that the aristocrat's greed and arrogance would continue to infect the blood of all subsequent Pyncheon heirs, leaving them forever unloved and aloof among their neighbors.

But even the worst blood thins out over a century and a half and Hepzibah and Clifford were already showing signs of being fed up with their heritage, ready to step out into a fresher relationship with the world around them. They were encouraged by a young cousin named Phoebe who had come to live with them. Still, it wasn't an easy exodus to achieve. Just consider Clifford. At 50 he despaired of laying aside the habits of decades. The best Phoebe could do was to bring him to an arched window on the second story to look from behind a curtain at the street life outside.

Slowly quite ordinary things began to stir his curiosity: a passing cab, an omnibus letting people on and off, a water cart, the howl of a locomotive. Then there was the fish cart, the vegetable cart, the organ grinder with a monkey dressed in highland plaid. But no experience widened Clifford's eyes so much as a passing parade one day with banners, drums, fifes, and cymbals. Clifford was so fascinated, he leaned out as if to baptize himself in that river of life, "to sink down and be covered by its profoundness, and then to emerge, sobered, invigorated, restored to the world and to himself." But his heritage still cautioned restraint!

It was only the following Sabbath experience that actually generated movement, what with the church bells ringing and the neighbors passing by in garments that "had the quality of ascension-robes." And there was Phoebe herself, exiting the old house with her green sunshade, throwing up a glance and a smile to Clifford and his sister in the arched window. So seduced were they by that smile and festive throng that Hepzibah cried out, "Dear brother, let us go!" Excitedly they put on their best old-fashioned clothes and descended the staircase. They pulled open the front door and started across the threshold—and then their hearts quaked within them. "It cannot be, Hepzibah!" said Clifford with deep sadness. "We are ghosts! We have no right anywhere, but in this old house which we are doomed to haunt."

What Nathaniel Hawthorne illustrates so well in his famous *The House of the Seven Gables* is how difficult it is for people to shake off the legacies and isolation of centuries. Look at what's been going on in Northern Ireland and between Serbs and Muslims, India and Pakistan, the genders, rich and poor, the political right and left. Unshakeable grudges, myths, self-righteousness keep them forever frozen in place. It's as though every nation, race, class, and sect were living within its own House of Seven Gables, reluctant to step out into a world where (as Saint Paul puts it in today's reading) Christ reveals the absurdity of the lethal, dated distinctions that keep us apart.

Neither Jew nor Greek, slave nor free, male nor female but all one Christic family! In this new millennium will that dream of Paul finally come true? Will humanity at long last be able to cry out as Clifford did when he finally escaped that haunted house: "Hepzibah, we can dance now!—we can sing, laugh, play. The weight is gone, Hepzibah; it is gone off this weary old world; and we may be as light-hearted as little Phoebe herself!"?

THIRTEENTH SUNDAY IN ORDINARY TIME

Galatians 5:1, 13–18

Christ Has Set Us Free!

There's a church in Rome called Saint Peter in Chains. It's built upon the site of the prison where Saint Peter was jailed prior to his execution by Nero. In its gift shop you can buy a few links of chain with a cross attached as a souvenir of your visit.

Of course, that wasn't the first time Peter found himself jailed. Shortly after Pentecost he was confined to an ecclesiastical prison in Jerusalem. It did no good, because that very night an angel let him out to preach again. So the next time Peter was arrested, they placed him in King Herod's more secure prison. Peter's hands and feet were chained and two guards assigned to share his cell, while two more sets of guards paced the corridors between his cell and the prison gate. But, as with James Cagney in those old 1930s movies, no slammer could hold Peter. Once again an angel appeared, put the guards to sleep, prodded Peter to get dressed, then escorted him to the gate that opened of its own accord.

I was discussing these episodes with a group of gentlemen who meet every week over scripture in the back room of Denny's Restaurant. And the question came up as to who this angel might be. Could it have been a friend on the prison staff? Or a visiting relative who, like Buster Keaton in the movie *Steamboat Bill,* may have carried into the jail a hollow loaf of French bread stuffed with the contents of a hardware store. But the "how" of such escapes is hardly relevant. The deeper question is: Why are so many such stories told throughout biblical and even secular literature?

I mean, as if two jail breaks weren't enough, we have a third later in the Acts of the Apostles in which Paul is a prisoner. Only this time it's an earthquake that opens up all the cell doors and flattens the prison walls—a funny outcome to everyone but the warden. And beyond Acts, think of all those other biblical accounts: Joseph's imprisonment and release, Jeremiah's confinement to a muddy cistern, Jonah's sojourn in the belly of a whale.

Or beyond the Bible, consider all those escape stories such as *The Count of Monte Cristo, The Prisoner of Zenda,* or those real or imagined escapes from Devil's Island or Alcatraz. Or remember that touching scene in Dickens's *A Tale of Two Cities* in which Sidney Carton (like Christ) sacrifices his own life to liberate Charles Darney. Or remember Tom Sawyer and Huckleberry Finn's hilarious effort to spring Jim loose from that cabin—or the emotion you feel when documentaries show American GIs opening the gates of Buchenwald to receive the tearful embraces of walking ghosts.

Why are we fascinated by such stories? I can only guess that deep down each one of us can identify with the inmates; each of us also feels somehow hobbled, handcuffed, confined. But by what? By fear, by some accuser or warden within our heads who sits in judgment upon us, who would have us doubt there is a God or any meaning to our lives and thereby drain us of all our energy, leaving us bilious and depressed—some demonic jailer who, though daffodils bloom all around us, would have us see only dungeon walls.

Isn't that why we are drawn to such stories? Because we, too, long for some angel to lift our spirits, to set us free—be it Mark Twain and his delightful duo Tom and Huck or the loving affirmation of a friend or some other agent of Christ, who summed up his mission in the words of Isaiah: The Spirit of the Lord is upon me . . . to bring glad tidings . . . to proclaim liberty to captives . . . to let the oppressed go free.

FOURTEENTH SUNDAY IN ORDINARY TIME

Galatians 6:14–18, John Donne, Rainer Maria Rilke

Beyond "God 101"

I thought I had finally arrived at a truly Christian understanding of God when, under the influence of the parables of Jesus and the writings of Saint Paul and Saint John, I began to think of God as more compassionate than judgmental. Up to that time I labored under an elementary school notion of God. I imagined him to be an eye in the sky, a perpetual watchman, surveying my very thoughts. I was under the impression he kept a book on me in which he tabulated and classified all my sins and would never erase them from his ledger unless I could convince him (or his priest) of a "firm purpose of amendment." Unfortunately, that was never firm enough to forestall my winding up in purgatory (at best), should I happen to die the following week. In other words, I grew up under the shadow of a celestial Accountant who passively brooded over me, making it quite clear that my salvation was in my own hands and that I'd better not drop the ball.

So it's no wonder that in my more mature years I welcomed those passages of the New Testament in which God is revealed to be a gracious parent, quick to understand and embrace me even as the father of the prodigal son—a God of empathy to whom I could relate candidly, intimately, without fear; in whose company I might at long last turn from morbid introspection to outward wonder and join him in creating a world.

But I was mistaken to think that with this more benign concept of God I had at last arrived at spiritual maturity. For there awaited me over the subsequent years of my life another more challenging experience of God—the experience Moses had one night when, as recorded in Exodus 4:24, the Lord met him on his return to Egypt and tried to kill him. Or the experience Jacob had one night by the Jabbok River, when something out of the darkness assaulted him and wrestled with him all night, leaving him at daybreak with his hip out of joint and grateful that he had seen God face to face and was still alive (see Genesis 32:23)!

Now what kind of a God is that, who lies in wait to do violence to us? Can this be a God of grace and mercy, who hits us with one contradiction after another, who gives our egos no rest, who would continually upset our complacency? But how else might a God who loves us seriously and passionately behave? A God who really cares about us will ultimately do everything he can to snap us out of the petulance, the arrogance, the deviousness, the timidity, the excuses that abort our becoming the radiant beings we are meant to be. He will work us over like a sculptor with mallet and steel, if necessary, to lay bare the beauty latent within us.

Of all the possible concepts of God available to us, it is this violently caring God whom the truly mature Christian finally adores—Christians like John Donne who in one of his sonnets pleads

> Batter my heart, three-personed God . . .
>   o'erthrow me, and bend
> Your force to break, blow, burn, and make me new . . .
>   for I,
> Except you enthrall me, shall never be free,
> Nor chaste, except you ravish me.[38]

Or people like Rainer Maria Rilke who wrote

> What we choose to fight is so tiny!
> What fights with us is so great! . . .

I mean the angel, who appeared
to the wrestlers of the Old Testament:
when the wrestler's sinews
grew long like metal strings,
he felt them under his fingers
like chords of deep music.

Whoever was beaten by this Angel . . .
went away proud and strengthened
and great from that harsh hand,
that kneaded him as if to change his shape.
Winning does not tempt that man.
This is how he grows: by being defeated, decisively,
by constantly greater beings.[39]

Anyone ready for an advanced course in "God"? Anyone ready, like Paul, to display the marks of Jesus upon one's body? Anyone ready to lose life in order to find it?

FIFTEENTH SUNDAY IN ORDINARY TIME

Luke 10:25–37, Film: Wrestling Ernest Hemingway

Tango

Thanks to the suggestion of a fellow parishioner, I watched a film called *Wrestling Ernest Hemingway* the other night. It takes place in Florida, where retirees abound. Richard Harris plays a resident of a seniors' motel by the ocean. He's 75 but won't admit it, doing push-ups, flexing his tattooed muscles. He's a loud ex-sailor, long-haired, unshaven, still a flirt. His son sends him a silly hat with visors front and back as a birthday present. Harris is hurt but bravado is his way of concealing pain.

And then there's Robert Duvall, who plays a retired Cuban-American barber with a pleasant Spanish accent. By contrast with Harris, Duvall is a quiet, dignified fellow who dresses casually but neatly. He has a set routine each day, stopping at a coffee shop to order a bacon sandwich and enjoy the presence of the waitress who serves him. He then spends time on a park bench carefully working a crossword puzzle, pausing on schedule to carefully unwrap and eat his bacon sandwich. It's here he meets Harris, who loudly intrudes upon Duvall's routine. Reluctantly at first but then patiently Duvall begins to socialize with Harris, always politely appalled at Harris's unkempt appearance and loud ways.

But soon his graceful manner begins to impact on Harris. The process comes to a climax when Duvall suggests that Harris do something about his shabby appearance and offers to give him a haircut and shave. Then occurs one of those beautiful moments in film. In Harris's run down apartment, Duvall has him sit down and puts a sheet around him. The camera then dwells upon his combing and snipping of Harris's hair, quietly and gently, around the ears and the back of the neck. You can sense Harris relaxing under the remote touch. Then we see Duvall honing his flat razor on a belt, back and forth slowly, testing the sharpness lightly with his thumb. Then we focus on the lather, the brush stirring in the foaming cup, the lather applied to Harris's face, applied by hand to the upper lip. And then, with a quiet, "I won't hurt you," Duvall begins to run the razor down Harris's cheek, under the chin—in soft, sure strokes. It's as though Duvall were sculpting a new man out of the old, a work of art, bringing out the latent beauty of an old man who misses his youth.

Having toweled away the excess lather, Duvall then goes to his barber's kit and pours a generous amount of aftershave lotion into his cupped hand. He bears it dripping to where Harris sits entranced and applies it carefully, firmly, slowly, affectionately massaging his cheeks and neck, his whole face. You can almost sense the experience yourself as you watch, smell the aroma and feel the sting.

It seems as though the scene lasts about fifteen minutes though it's no doubt less. And as Harris emerges from the experience, a fine looking, smooth, peaceful man instead of loud extrovert, you realize you have just been mesmerized by the performance of an ordinary, everyday deed—a haircut and shave—but performed by a man of grace and majesty (like the Good Samaritan?) who has turned this ordinary deed into a quiet ballet. No need for special effects or the usual "shoot-'em-up" finale or a bedroom scene cliché. This scene, similar in wonder to the French dinner prepared and served in *Babette's Feast*, should be memorable long after Rambo has become as dated as Hopalong Cassidy.

When the video came to an end (even though I'm already old) I knew what I want to be when I grow up: a man of grace who deals with himself and others and a bacon sandwich the way Duvall does—with pride, reverence, dignity, and a style reflective of the gracious, divine artist who made me—a man of grace who dances life in the stately way Duvall dances the Tango at the film's end.

SIXTEENTH SUNDAY IN ORDINARY TIME

Luke 10:38–42

One Thing Only Is Required

When Jesus launched the church to broadcast his gospel through-out the world, he knew he was taking a risk. He knew that, with human nature being what it is, his message would be muted by things like pomposity, party strife, even by success and the wealth that comes of success! Indeed, by the sixteenth century the church had become so opulent, one could hardly preach on "Blessed are the poor" without provoking a snicker throughout the congregation. Then there was the risk of bureaucracy. And sure enough, it wasn't long before the simple organization of the early church grew into an administrative pyramid so high and mighty, it made the ordinary peasant feel more distant from God than ever.

But it was something you'd least suspect that may have undercut the gospel's impact on humanity most of all. At some point in time, the church lost its nerve, lowered its aim, and chose to put most of its resources into making people virtuous instead of marvelous.

We see Jesus anticipating this tendency and having to deal firmly with it in today's gospel reading. He's visiting Martha and Mary and Martha is the busy one, being very hospitable, dutiful, and virtuous. Mary, on the other hand, is doing nothing. She's "wasting time" from a virtuous person's point of view. She's just sitting there mesmerized by Jesus' vision of life and reality. Martha complains, "Jesus, tell Mary to make herself useful!" But Jesus says, in effect, "Settle down, Martha. Mary has chosen to remain under my spell, my God-spell, which will energize her soon enough, not in the frantic, worried, duty-bound way you're behaving, but grace-fully, beautifully, creatively, quietly, softly, truly, as befits someone under my spell."

We see Jesus having to make this same point again in John 12:1–8 and its parallel reading in Mark 14:3–9 toward the end of his life. He is once more a guest with his disciples in the home of Martha and Mary. And Martha is as virtuous as ever, waiting on everybody, making sure the forks and knives and napkins are prop-erly placed. And what's Mary doing? Nothing very useful, actually something very wasteful! She empties a flask of rich perfume over the feet of Jesus, massages them leisurely and wipes them with her hair, filling the house with the fragrance of her deed. "What a waste!" says Judas. "How much more virtuous it would have been to sell that perfume and donate the proceeds to some charity." Mere pro-priety seeks precedence over grandeur, extravagance, *beau geste.* Jesus sees what's happening and rebukes Judas. "Leave her alone!" he says. "She has done a beautiful thing."

When you begin to think about it, we didn't need Jesus to teach us about virtue, defined as "righteousness and responsibility, probity, conformity to standard morality, rectitude, abstention from vices." Long before he ever came along we had plenty of Hebrew scribes to promote that. We also had all those Greek and Roman philosophers, the Stoics, to teach us about prudence, justice, temperance, and fortitude, about moral equilibrium. Jesus came to lift us an infinite distance higher, to challenge us to become splendid human beings, capable of unexpected, beautiful, not just prosaically proper behavior.

But somewhere in the past we lost our nerve. Looking at raw human nature, we concluded that "the potential for beauty there is pretty slim. We'll be lucky if we can keep humanity's head above water." And so, putting the gospel on hold, we fell back upon the modest expectations and moralizing of the scribes and Stoics. We chose the Pax Romana instead of Shalom. And Jesus wept— because the whole point of his gospel is: it's not enough to be dutiful; we can and must be beautiful.

SEVENTEENTH SUNDAY IN ORDINARY TIME

Colossians 2:12–14, Edgar Allan Poe

And the Beat Goes On

Edgar Allan Poe[40] was fascinated with premature burials, with characters who felt some need to bury people alive. For instance, there's the story entitled "The Cask of Amontillado" in which, for some past slight, Montresor invites Fortunato to descend to his cellar to sample a special wine. There Montresor chains his guest to the back wall of an alcove and slowly seals up the opening with masonry. "I forced the last stone into its position; I plastered it up. *In pace requiescat.*" Then there's the character Roderick in "The Fall of the House of Usher" who prematurely entombs his twin sister in a basement vault, only to hear the vault's iron door clang open, to hear her footsteps on the stairs, to behold her standing enshrouded on the threshold of his study!

And then there's "The Tell-Tale Heart." Of all the movies and plays I've seen in my lifetime, my high school's dramatization of that Poe tale remains memorable to me—particularly its special effects. You know the story. The main character couldn't stand the presence of an old man who shared his house. "One of his eyes," he complains, "resembled that of a vulture—a pale blue eye. . . . Whenever it fell on me, my blood ran cold; and so by degrees . . . I made up my mind . . . to rid myself of the eye forever." So he did away with the old fellow, took up the floorboards, deposited the corpse, and "replaced the boards so cleverly, so cunningly, that no human eye—not even *his*—could have detected anything wrong."

No sooner had he finished the task than three policemen knocked at his door responding to a neighbor's report of a scream during the night. "I bade them search—search *well*," he says, for he was quite confident no trace of the deed would be found. Except that, while he conversed with the police, a low, dull, quick sound began to pulsate throughout the room.

This is where our special effects crew riveted the audience's attention. From a low, barely perceptible thump, thump, thump, thump to an ever-louder THUMP, THUMP, THUMP, THUMP, the buried heart echoed throughout the theater—while the main character became increasingly mad! "O God! What could I do? I foamed—I raved—I swore! I swung the chair upon which I had been sitting, and grated it upon the boards, but the noise continually increased. . . . I felt that I must scream or die!"

Beyond mere entertainment, Poe had a far deeper intent in telling such stories. Some think he was anticipating modern materialism's effort over the past 200 years to bury both God and the human heart—to evaluate everything in terms of "profitability" and to repress such things as conscience and sentiment as romantic nonsense—to bury them well beneath the floor boards of our psyche so as not to impede "progress." But note how in most of these stories the beat goes on! The buried person revives, even as God and the human heart will revive, no matter how much a cynical society would stifle their influence.

In such stories Poe stands well within our gospel tradition, which pivots upon another premature burial—the attempt of a totalitarian empire to entomb Christ, only to be foiled by his resurrection on the third day. And what was Christ's resurrection but an overture to our own resurrection every time Christ summons us (as he summoned Lazarus from his tomb) to emerge from all that would suffocate our bigness of mind and heart?

Could it be that, consciously or unconsciously, all those Poe stories were ultimately influenced by passages like today's second reading from Saint Paul? "You were buried with him in baptism . . . you were also raised with him through faith in the power of God, who raised him from the dead" (Colossians 2:12).

EIGHTEENTH SUNDAY IN ORDINARY TIME

Ecclesiastes 1:2; 2:21–23, Emily Dickinson, R. S. Thomas, Denise Levertov

Depressed?

We read a Sunday selection from Ecclesiastes only once every three years. Why is that? Maybe because it's not as upbeat as other biblical works. Indeed, the rabbis of 2,000 years ago hesitated for a long time to include it in the Bible. Its tone was so skeptical, as is evident in passages like: "What has been will be and what has been done will be done again; there is nothing new under the sun" (Ecclesiastes 1:9, author's translation). Eventually they did vote it in, possibly because they realized even believers get depressed and Ecclesiastes offers them a way to vent their frustration.

And by the way, that opening line "Vanity of vanities! All things are vanity!" doesn't capture in modern English the actual despondency of the speaker. Today the word vanity suggests excessive pride or conceit. In the original Hebrew the line reads more like: "A wisp of breath, mere mist! All is transient vapor!" In other words: Life and reality have no more substance than a passing cloud. How's that for despondent?

And yet so many of us can identify with that sense of futility as jobs keep changing and the kids grow up too fast and memories fade and even the most sublime literature tastes flat and we're not sure who's president and don't even care and God seems so silent and remote. One could say Ecclesiastes is especially attuned to our era, because today (perhaps more than ever) people seem confused about the meaning of life and so many plays and poems express malaise. A good example is Emily Dickinson's poem:

> A Pit—but Heaven over it—
> And Heaven beside, and Heaven abroad,
> And yet a Pit—
> With Heaven over it.
>
> To stir would be to slip—
> To look would be to drop—
> To dream–to sap the Prop
> That holds my chances up.
> Ah! Pit! with Heaven over it![41]

And then there is R. S. Thomas, the Anglican priest and poet who lived in Wales until his death in 2000 at the age of 87. He, too, was at times oppressed by the silence of God:

> The relation between us was
> silence . . .
> It had begun

> by my talking all of the time
> repeating the worn formulae
> of the churches in the belief
> that was prayer. Why does silence
> suggest disapproval?
> The prattling
> ceased, not suddenly but,
> as flowers die off in a frost
> my requests thinned. I contented
> myself I was answering
> his deafness with dumbness. My tongue
> lolled, clapper of a disused
> bell that would never again
> pound on him.[42]

But I wonder whether it's not at such moments when things go blank, when we're reduced to silence, no longer able to pray, with no more props to lean on or straws to grasp—I wonder if it isn't precisely then that God is closest to us, silent though he be—but tangible as breath, glad at last that all our assumptions have been laid to rest and we can let go, allow ourselves to fall into his quiet, mysterious presence. That's what Denise Levertov (in her poem "Suspended") once felt when very much in the mood of Ecclesiastes:

> I had grasped God's garment in the void
> but my hand slipped
> on the rich silk of it.
> The 'everlasting arms' my sister loved to remember
> must have upheld my leaden weight
> from falling, even so,
> for though I claw at empty air and feel
> nothing, no embrace,
> I have not plummetted.[43]

NINETEENTH SUNDAY IN ORDINARY TIME

Romans 9:1–5, Isaac Rosenberg

How Odd of God

High over the portals within the south transept of the 800-year-old cathedral of Chartres in France spreads a great Rose window, forty feet in diameter. At its center sits Christ, while immediately around him orbit eight angels and symbols for the four evangelists, each enclosed within a circle of stained glass—and beyond them orbit the 24 elders of the book of Revelation, each also within its own bejeweled circle—for a total of 36 orbiting circles of blue, red, gold, purple, and white! Enough to make your head spin. Nor is that gigantic wheel of color the only thing to enchant you in that soaring wing of the cathedral, because below it rise five more long and narrow windows, the central one featuring Mary, while the other four show images of the evangelists, Luke and Matthew, John, and Mark—in that sequence.

Now if you look closely at the four windows of the evangelists, you'll notice something amusing. Each evangelist, appearing almost boyish in size, sits on the shoulders of a tall prophet of the Old Testament: Luke on the shoulders of Jeremiah, Matthew on Isaiah's, John on Ezekiel's, and Mark on Daniel's. The four major voices of the New Testament ride piggyback on the four major voices of the Old—just the way your daddy lifted you high on his shoulders for a towering view of the world when you where a little child. Why would those artists do something as playful as that? Well, it wasn't playful. They wanted to make a serious point, namely that the gospels build on the wisdom and vision of the Hebrew Bible. Christianity rides on the shoulders of Judaism!

We tend to forget that. But the astounding truth is, Western civilization draws its dynamism from the legends and history and poetry and wisdom of a small Middle Eastern nation that politically never amounted to anything near the size and power of the empires that surrounded it. And where are those empires today: ancient Babylon, Egypt, Assyria, the empires of Alexander the Great and the Caesars? Gone with but the feeblest echo compared to the impact of little Israel upon this planet. From the Jewish people came not only Abraham, Rachel, Moses, Miriam, David, Solomon, Esther, and Ruth, but also a girl named Mary, whose image is central to every Catholic church on every continent throughout the world, and her son, whose gospel continues to irritate every selfish soul to this very day. And then there were Peter and Paul and those earliest Christians, who were courageous Jews.

You don't have to be a believer to conclude that little Israel's influence on every other ethnic group in this world has been miraculously profound and widespread. And that's what the makers of the windows of Chartres were trying to depict: how our church rides on the shoulders of the saints and visionaries of a Semitic people whose spiritual stature has helped us to see farther into the origins and destiny of human existence. And yet, how often among the very nations that worshipped in such cathedrals were the Jewish people treated as odd, alien, sinister, scapegoats for every rabble-rouser to abuse.

And so we need to pay more attention to what those artists of Chartres were trying to say. We need to remember that it was not "odd of God to choose the Jews" but mysteriously in keeping with his plan to redeem us all from lethal ignorance. We need to take to heart the lament of a Jewish poet, Isaac Rosenberg, who wrote in his poem, "The Jew":[44]

> Moses, from whose loins I sprung,
> Lit by a lamp in his blood
> Ten immutable rules, a moon
> For mutable lampless men.

The blond, the bronze, the ruddy,
With the same heaving blood,
Keep tide to the moon of Moses.
Then why do they sneer at me?

TWENTIETH SUNDAY IN ORDINARY TIME

Jeremiah 38:4–6, 8–11, Mark Twain

The Cave

We live in a world of many objects: stars, oceans, trees, birds, flowers, and rivers. For the scientist they are phenomena to be studied or analyzed in terms of their make up: molecules, atoms, and so on. But for poets, both biblical and otherwise, they are all reflections of ourselves—metaphors through which we may better understand ourselves and our destiny.

Consider a cave. Caves fascinate us. *National Geographic* once did a TV show on cave exploration. I couldn't take my eyes off it as the camera moved through narrow corridors into cathedral-like vaults full of those conical drippings. You felt like Pinocchio in the belly of a whale. And then there are all those juvenile books entitled *The Endless Dark* or *The Underground Episode*. They all begin with children discovering a dark opening and entering, then losing their way. Their candles burn out and they are plunged in darkness; they call out and hear only their echoes. The classic cave experience is that of Tom Sawyer where he and Becky find themselves in such a predicament, where the story says their "call went echoing down the empty aisles and died out in the distance in a faint sound that resembled a ripple of mocking laughter."[45]

In such stories, at a deeper level, I think the authors are suggesting we identify with the children. Not infrequently in life we ourselves descend into some tunnel, become buried in some cave where we find no light, only loneliness, silence—no way out. For some people it was school—all those years of drudgery before graduation. For some it's the period after the loss of a loved one, when we go groping through one dim day after another. For others, it's an illness (ours or that of a family member) that closes in on us, giving us no latitude to enjoy life as we once did. For others it's a state of mind, a depression or despair that grips us. We call out and no one notices, no one can hear, no one apparently cares.

Oh, there are moments of hope as with Tom and Becky:

> "Tom!"
>
> "Well, Becky?"
>
> "They'll miss us and hunt for us!"
>
> "Yes, they will! . . . "
>
> "Maybe they are hunting for us now, Tom. . . ."
>
> By and by, Tom said:
>
> "*Sh!* Did you hear that?"
>
> Both held their breath and listened. There was a sound like the faintest far-off shout. . . .
>
> "It's them!" said Tom, "they're coming!"

But then the sound fades or was it only an illusion? And we remain lost like Tom and Becky in their cave or like Lazarus and Jesus in their tombs, which amounts to the same thing.

Yet somehow the characters keep hoping and working to find their way out. There's something in each of us, call it God's Spirit, that keeps us going. Tom "followed two avenues as far as his kite line would stretch." He "followed a third to the fullest stretch of the kite line, and was about to turn back when he glimpsed a far off speck that looked like daylight." Tom went back for Becky and "she almost died for joy when she had groped to where she actually saw the blue speck of daylight." And making his way, Tom finally "pushed his head and shoulders through a small hole, and saw the broad Mississippi rolling by!"

What does that say about where you are now spiritually? Is it a pretty good reflection of the course of your own life at times? That's why we read stories or study metaphors: to find out about ourselves and cultivate hope that we, too, may emerge from the cave or cistern in which we find ourselves—to catch at least a glimpse of that great river Tom beheld, which is nothing less than the river of life-giving water shown by an angel to the visionary John in the book of Revelation: "sparkling like crystal, flowing from the throne of God and of the Lamb" (Revelation 22:1).

TWENTY-FIRST SUNDAY IN ORDINARY TIME

Luke 13:22–33

Exit by the Narrow Gate

In today's reading from Luke, Jesus warns us that the gateway to heaven may not only be a tight squeeze but actually locked by the time we consider entering. And it won't be enough to be simply a card-carrying Christian to get in. That's a depressing thought for a summer afternoon. But I think we may better understand what Jesus is saying in Luke if we shift over to chapter seven of Matthew's gospel where he makes a similar remark: "Enter by the narrow gate, for the road is wide that leads to destruction and many there are who take that route; while the gate to life is so tight and its path so narrow that few can even find it."

Now notice how Matthew locates that remark right after Jesus' long sermon on the mount where he actually describes the tight behavioral path down which he would lead us to fullness of life. Let me paraphrase it for you: "Hold no grudges. Don't obsess over offenses. Stop nursing your anger. Don't sneer at anyone for, as far as I'm concerned, it's equivalent to murder! See in every woman you meet the unique, precious person she is. Don't reduce her to a consumable object. Don't be so litigious. Don't get caught up in the paranoia of fine print. When you say yes, mean yes; when you say no, mean no. Be candid, trusting, and trustworthy. Don't think of getting even. If somebody rips you off, send him a gratuity. Give and forgive as extravagantly as God gives and forgives. Love not cautiously but adventurously, seeing potential friendship even among people who despise you. Make money a means, not an end. As an alternative to the *Wall Street Journal,* look for the immense dividends that await you in the book of Job, the gospel of John, or the tragedies of Shakespeare. Stop worrying. Let go and let God. And pass no judgment. Take the speck out of your own eye before assuming to become your brother's oculist."

Now compare that to the broad, reckless, alternative behavioral freeway people prefer in order not so much to live as to survive: "Never let go of a grudge or forget an injury. Treat women as second-class citizens. Litigate at the drop of a hat! Avoid simple solutions. If you can make things complex, do so by all means. Don't get mad; get even. Demand an eye for an eye, a tooth for a tooth, or (better still) a million dollar settlement for a fender bender. If you don't like someone, brood, savor your hatred, salivate over his downfall. Forget about pie in the sky; money in the bank is what matters. For your daily spiritual reading, study the stock market. And by all means, worry! Worry about clothes, food, school, retirement, and the Dow. And never let a day go by without evaluating others, ferreting out the faults of X, smirking at the ignorance of Y, gossiping over the lechery of Z—all the while, of course, maintaining a proper, pious facade yourself."

There's the wide-open, hell-bent way society's pundits encourage us to live by and survive—the behavioral freeway where everyone must race to stay ahead and passing on the right is fine if you can get away with it and cursing the slowpoke ahead of you comes naturally, especially if you're provoked by some demagogue's voice issuing from your dashboard.

So, given the popularity of Broadway, it's no wonder Jesus sounds pessimistic about anyone ever negotiating the simple exit he offers us to fullness of life—or about even a nominal Christian getting past its toll booth—because, you see, the odd and difficult thing about Jesus' narrow gate is we have to be very "BIG" to get through, whereas all Broadway requires is that we remain comfortably "small."

TWENTY-SECOND SUNDAY IN ORDINARY TIME

Luke 14:1, 7–14

He Spoke a Parable to Those Who Were Invited

I heard recently that the *Ave Maria Hour* is on the air again, on one station only, in Poughkeepsie, New York. Does anyone remember the *Ave Maria Hour*? It was broadcast weekly on over four hundred radio stations across the country from 1935 to 1945. It opened with Gounod's "Ave Maria," followed by a full dramatization of some saint's life. There was no preaching, no long lecture by some clergyman. Only a good script read by professional actors with music and sound effects. It was quite popular among Catholics and others as well. I was only a kid but I listened to it as faithfully as I listened to *The Lone Ranger* and *Captain Midnight.*

It's nice to know they're pulling those old transcriptions out of the vault and airing them again. Indeed, it's wise to do so, because stories are so much more effective than lectures or catechisms when it comes to communicating what Christianity is all about. God seems to think so since his basic book, the Bible, is full of drama and episodes that have held people's attention for close to 4,000 years.

I mean, when I went to parochial school and later to the seminary, the church had two methods of teaching us about God and Christ and human origins and destiny. On the one hand there were the catechism and theological tomes full of big Mary Poppins words like hyperdulia, hypostatic, and supererogation! On the other hand, there were those biblical accounts about Jonah, Noah, Elisha, David and Goliath, and Jesus walking on the water. Beyond that, there were stories of Saint Francis preaching to the birds, Saint Anthony preaching to the fishes, and Saint John Bosco cracking walnuts between his thumb and forefinger. Guess which approach impressed us most! The stories, of course. The lives of the saints, which began by fascinating us and then lifted us beyond our petty horizons toward visions of heroism.

Stories remind us of how our church began. They remind us that we are not simply an institution (the product of some corporate executives) but an extended family, descended from a nomad named Abraham and his descendants. As a church, we originated among a pastoral people who lived in tents much like the Sioux and Arapahoe, a tribe, a family that survived on storytelling, that perpetuated its identity and values by a grandmother's repeating inspiring, tragic, and sometimes comical events—about how Abraham once made a big mistake by moving to the big city and almost lost his wife as well as his shirt; about how some uncles did their kid brother Joseph wrong, only to have the kid brother later save their skins.

You can identify with that, can't you? Doesn't the same thing go on in your family, stories told by uncles and aunts that make you laugh or cry or both? Recently, with the death of my mother and several aunts, my sister and I found ourselves thrown into their vacated storyteller role almost by reflex—as we sat in a living room with nephews and nieces and cousins, enhancing tales of experiences we ourselves had heard a hundred times. It's beautiful. It's warm. It's nurturing. It's family.

Which is why I like the project recently thought up by my parish's youth ministry, asking us all to submit a personal story for a parish publication—something about a moment of discovery, pain, joy; about hilarious or moving experiences—you name it! The point? Maybe by sharing such stories we'll get to know each other better—and treasure each other. Maybe we'll begin to become an extended family after all. That's what stories tend to do: create a sense of family. And that's what our church is supposed to be.

TWENTY-THIRD SUNDAY IN ORDINARY TIME

Philemon 9b–10, 12–17, A. N. Wilson

Regarding Philemon

How did the letter to Philemon get into the New Testament? It's nothing more than a 23-line letter of reference in which Paul asks Philemon to treat leniently a runaway slave named Onesimus. Why would the church include a seemingly trivial note within its collection of Paul's otherwise lengthy and theologically weighty epistles?

The letter dates from around the year 63 when Paul was under arrest in Rome. He was old and worn out, when along came this Onesimus, who probably met him during one of Paul's visits to Philemon's home in Asia Minor. We may speculate that, having become a fugitive slave, Onesimus sought refuge with Paul and became so devoted a servant that Paul refers to him in the letter as "my child" and "my own heart."

Now slavery was taken for granted back in ancient Rome. And so it's not surprising that even affluent Christians like Philemon would possess them. Nor could it be easily abolished without catastrophic consequences similar to those faced by America as recently as the 1790s. In his book *Founding Brothers* Joseph Ellis describes the debate that took place even then to abolish

slavery as incompatible with the principles of the American
Revolution. But the southern states resisted the idea and argued,
"Rice cannot be brought to market without these people." And so,
even among these Christian lawmakers the issue of slavery had to
be tabled lest the South withdraw from the Union at a time when
our Federal government was too new and fragile to prevent it.

But at least by the 1790s, after almost two millennia of
Christian civilization, slavery had become an embarrassment. The
same could not be said of ancient Rome nor did the early church
itself agitate politically to abolish it. And yet its very baptismal ritual
was about as subversive a practice as you could imagine, because
the early church was open to people from all ranks and classes; and
once they were baptismally immersed in Christ and made eligible
to gather around the table of the Lord, all their secular distinctions
were laid aside. It didn't matter whether by society's standards they
were Jew or Greek, male or female, slave or free; they were now
simply brothers and sisters within God's family, forerunners of
a redeemed and united human race.

This is so evident in Paul's letter to Philemon in which Paul
can ask (and even command) Philemon to receive Onesimus back
"no longer as a slave, but more than a slave, a brother, beloved especially to me, but even more so to you, as a man and in the Lord"
(verse 16). The Emperor Nero might soon execute Paul but he had
no way of stopping letters like this from passing through his postal
service to lay the foundation of future revolutions whose slogans
would proclaim liberty, fraternity, equality. So maybe the presence
of this letter in the New Testament is not so strange after all.

And yet there may be a more specific reason for its being
there. In his recent biography of Paul, A. N. Wilson notes that years
after Paul wrote the letter, a bishop named Ignatius (while en route
to Rome to face trial and execution) wrote to the Christians of
Ephesus, encouraging fidelity to their bishop. That bishop's name
was Onesimus. And so Wilson suggests, "It is not too far-fetched,

surely, to suppose that the slave boy convert of the apostle Paul should, in his venerable old age, have become the Father in Christ of the Ephesian church? And more than that, scholars have concluded that it was likely this Onesimus who was largely responsible for preserving and editing the body of Paul's letters. If this were the case, it would certainly explain why the letter to Philemon has been preserved to us."[46] Bishop Onesimus had a personal interest in its inclusion!

TWENTY-FOURTH SUNDAY IN ORDINARY TIME

Luke 15:1–32, William Wordsworth

The Good Shepherd

In his poem called "Michael,"[47] William Wordsworth tells of an eighteenth-century shepherd in England's mountain country who had a son in his old age. Over his growing years the old shepherd taught him lovingly all there was to know about pasturing. Alone for days together on the mountain slopes, the two became profoundly close.

And then one day along came bad news. A relative had defaulted on a loan. The shepherd had been a co-signer and was now liable for it. The only solution lay in the son's going off to London to work off the debt. On the day before his departure the father took the son to a quiet meadow where he had intended to build a stone sheepfold. He asked his son to lay the first stone, a kind of cornerstone, as a way of recalling his son to mind while he was away:

> Now, fare thee well—
> When thou return'st, thou in this place wilt see
> A work which is not here, a covenant

'Twill be between us—but whatever fate
Befall thee, I shall love thee to the last . . .

Off went the young man and for a long while he wrote
cheerful letters—and then silence! He had fallen in with bad company and eventually sailed off to some distant continent, never to
be seen again. The poem then tells of the father's thereafter visiting
that unfinished sheepfold every day until he died, but whether he
went to complete the work or simply to grieve we'll never know—
although some people believed

That many and many a day he thither went,
And never lifted up a single stone.

Now that's a sad story and if I had my druthers, in a situation like that I'd rather follow the example of the shepherd in Jesus'
parable, who upon losing one of his sheep, did not despair but
left the other ninety nine to find it and upon finding it carried it
home rejoicing. Indeed, I actually do identify more with Jesus' shepherd, because, not unlike so many other parents who lose a child
to this or that influence, I, too, lost a child.

I might have foreseen his going astray ever since the day
he got under the fence at the end of our property when he was still
a toddler and disappeared for a frantic hour or two. Thereafter it
seemed we were always climbing one fence after another to track
him down, because he seemed always fascinated by the enticements
that lay beyond the boundaries of proper behavior. And so I followed him into Haight Asbury and up Highway Five to Oregon and
in the wake of the Sonoma Airport Express ferrying passengers to
San Francisco International in the early morning mist (upon finding his room empty once more). And I kept finding him and bringing him home (me rejoicing, him not)—only to be on the road
again, until, when he turned 19 we arrived at an understanding.
He would go his way and I would go mine and we'd meet in between,

which we did peacefully and laughingly until I began to realize we had finally found each other after all, not on my terms, not on terms suitable to this world's standards, but heart to heart, not just as frantic father and lost son, but as relaxed friends.

And in the process, you know what? I found someone else. I found myself, the me that cares enough to go to the end of the world for someone. My lost sheep had brought out the Good Shepherd within me!—the me who once feigned or repressed caring until this wayward lamb brought out the passion, the heart, the tears, and the Christ in me.

He went under another fence nine years ago this month. Try as I might, it's hard for me to follow him there—until such time as our ultimate Good Shepherd gathers me too into that ultimate fold where neither time nor space nor death can ever separate us again.

TWENTY-FIFTH SUNDAY IN ORDINARY TIME

Luke 16:1–13

The Logic of Desperation: Do Something!

People find the apparent moral of today's gospel parable a bit questionable. It seems to congratulate an employee for being dishonest. Here's a fellow who has mismanaged his employer's accounts, costing him tons of money. The employer gives him two weeks notice and what does the fellow do but use the time to rip him off—to insure his own future security. Does the employer call the cops? No! He actually compliments the employee for doing whatever he had to do to survive—and Jesus seems to share the employer's admiration. Well, Jesus or no Jesus, any parochial school nun in my day would have given the fellow a swat!

But was his deed immoral? Perhaps the employee was an early socialist who felt his employer's superfluous wealth needed redistribution. Or consider two modern versions of the same parable:

Version 1: A computer expert works for Microsoft and is privy to the corporation's advanced technology. But his efficiency is poor and his salary too big; so the company puts him on the list for downsizing. Before the pink slip arrives he contacts a competitor and offers to share everything he knows about Microsoft. Bingo! He soon becomes an affluent Vice President of the other company. Now, given the loose standards prevailing in our free enterprise system, how many people would condemn the fellow? Indeed, many would probably praise him for (and I put it euphemistically) causing Bill Gates discomfort.

Version 2: Dimitri was a Soviet rocket scientist during the Cold War. He was intimately involved in the Soviet Union's military and space industry. Because of a cost overrun in his program, he fell into disfavor. Promotion was out of the question. He actually anticipated a transfer to Siberia. Along comes a CIA agent. Dimitri offers to reveal everything he knows about the Soviet missile program if the agent can get him out of the country. The agent does so, and Dimitri and his family wind up in a posh home (at a six-figure salary) in Huntsville, Alabama, and later he becomes a Fellow at the Hoover Institute. Would you, as a patriotic American, condemn Dimitri's behavior? Or would you say, "Golly, what a courageous fellow. He deserves a medal"?

So you see, the morality of the central character in such stories is arguable. But ultimately it doesn't matter, because the focus of the story is not on the morality of what the fellow does but on how he behaved in a desperate situation! He didn't just sit there; he did something radical to save his life.

This is precisely what Christ would have us do when one morning we wake up in a cold sweat, desperately aware of how shallow we've become; when we wake up to the fact that we've been living monotonously from day to day instead of deliberately and poetically; when we realize how much we've allowed our minds to be trashed by the gossip and paranoia of the media, the din of commercials, the gospel of materialism; when we recall we haven't had a profound conversation with anyone in years.

Then it's time to do something radical—like buy a ticket to *King Lear* or listen to the lyrics of Handel's *Messiah* or study the book of Job and Paul's letter to the Romans—time to find out what sacrament means and in what way we ourselves are sacraments— time to find out what eucharist means and learn to feed better on that weekly experience. In a word, it's time to acquire depth: the peace, wonder, and energy that derive from a more profoundly spiritual way of being.

TWENTY-SIXTH SUNDAY IN ORDINARY TIME

1 Timothy 6:11–16, Virgil

Time to Catch a Second Wind

In Virgil's epic *The Aeneid*,[48] the gods must resort to sending a celestial messenger to prod Aeneas to pursue his destiny. "Are you forgetful of what is your own kingdom, your own fate? . . . what are you pondering or hoping for . . . squandering your ease in Libyan lands?" According to Virgil, the gods helped Aeneas and his followers escape the fall of ancient Troy so that they might one day build a new Troy in Italy. So Aeneas has no right to be dillydally-ing in seductive Dido's North African boudoir. He and his posterity must be faithful to their mission: to tame the wildness of men that brought about the fall of Troy, to force aimless and barbaric nations to submit to a rule of reason and law, and thus to harness all that energy to produce not devastation but universal order and prosperity. The mission of Aeneas and the new Troy (to be named Rome) was to civilize the known world. That, at least, was stoical Virgil's vision of his nation's destiny.

Just as often in biblical lore the God of the Hebrews finds it necessary to prod Abraham and his descendents to be faithful to their destiny. In the book of Genesis, Abraham is called by God to leave aggressive and avaricious Babel to generate a better world. But soon Abraham begins to fret, to doubt that he can father a nobler human race. His descendents, too, grow weary of this quest. Nostalgic for the immediate comforts of tyrannical Egypt, they complain, "Why have you brought us into this wilderness?" And continually God must rumble and lecture and challenge them to "keep the faith." Ultimately this God of the Hebrews sends Jesus to revive human commitment to Abraham's dream. Joining our historical procession he takes the lead saying, "Come, follow me, oh ye of little faith. No one who puts his hand to the plow and looks back is fit for the kingdom of God."

America is heir to the quests of Aeneas, Abraham, and all those men and women of faith who were convinced life does have meaning, that is, that we have a destiny larger than ourselves to pursue. Such faith is often ridiculed nowadays. Skepticism and agnosticism are fashionable. "Enlightened" people aren't taken in by naïve idealism or religious "illusions." Of course, the inevitable consequence of such "enlightenment" is the ruthless ethic of "me first" and "go for it." Why live for anything but my own short-term profit and self-interest? And so we have instances of a Material Girl usurping the name and pedestal of the Madonna.

And yet today reminders of these inherited visions remain spread across the landscape of America—with towns and villages called Troy, Rome, Athens, Ithaca, Cicero, Cato, and Cincinatti, reminding us of our Greco-Roman dream of a rational, disciplined, equitable society, superior to every form of tyranny or barbarism, a vision revived by the founders of this republic. And then there are those other American towns called Bethel, Shiloh, Mount Zion, Mount Gilead, Jericho, Bethlehem, Nazareth, Bethany, New Hope, and Paradise that remind us of our Hebrew heritage, that vision held by Abraham and Christ of a society not simply rational and equitable but irrationally generous, gracious and compassionate in the manner of Christ—the kind of society our church is meant to display.

Still, reminders are often not enough to counter the doubts we sometimes have of attaining so sublime a destiny. We grow weary, and we begin to agree with the "smart" people that life may have no meaning. And so God must intervene again as he does in today's second reading in which Saint Paul confronts Timothy and you and me down this latter stretch of the year, saying: "Pursue righteousness, devotion, faith, love, patience and gentleness. Compete well for the faith. Lay hold of eternal life, to which you were called . . . in the presence of may witnesses" (1 Timothy 6:11–12).

TWENTY-SEVENTH SUNDAY IN ORDINARY TIME

Habakkuk 1:2–3; 2:2–4, Lewis Carroll

If I Wasn't Real, I Shouldn't Be Able to Cry

When Lewis Carroll's Alice[49] stepped into the looking glass one day, she found herself in a landscape laid out like a chessboard. Assigned the role of a white pawn, she was required to make her way square by square to the top of the board where, if she survived, she would be crowned a Queen. When she arrived at square four, she met two chubby and identical brothers called Tweedledum and Tweedledee.

They enjoyed contradicting each other in much the way Republicans and Democrats do. Tweedledum's favorite response was "Nohow!" to be met by Tweedledee's "Contrariwise!" But for all their seeming opposition they only amounted to opposite ends of the same contrary spectrum like the Tweedledums and Tweedledees you see on Crossfire and other such shows.

Now it so happened that Alice heard something like a steam engine puffing away. Tweedledee told her it was only the Red King snoring under a tree in the next square. "Come and look at him! . . . Isn't he a *lovely* sight?" said the brothers. And there he was sound asleep in all his regalia. "He's dreaming now," said Tweedledee, "and what do you think he's dreaming about?" Alice couldn't guess. "Why, about *you!*" said Tweedledee. "And if he left off dreaming about you, where do you suppose you'd be?" Alice protested she'd be right where she was. "Not you!" replied Tweedledee. "You'd be nowhere. Why you're only a sort of thing in his dream!" Tweedledum then put in his two cents: "If that King was to wake, you'd go out—bang—just like a candle!"

Well, Alice became indignant. She insisted she did exist independently of the King's dream. But did she? Do we? There are thinkers who suggest that this universe and everything in it may only be the dream or fantasy of some cosmic creator that may disappear when he wakes up or chooses no longer to think about us. It's a way of saying we may be without any substance whatsoever.

Of course, we take it for granted we are real and important beings. But there may be an element of truth in Tweedledee's suggestion, for how many people down through history have in fact lived out their lives as pawns in somebody else's dream: the soldiers of Napoleon, fulfilling his imperial ambitions; the citizens of Germany marching to the tune of fascism; the many children compelled to fulfill the dream their parents have for them. But something in us resents the thought much the way Alice resented Tweedledee's teasing. "I *am* real," she said and then began to cry. "You won't make yourself a bit realer by crying!" insisted Tweedledee.

And here Alice strikes a telling blow; she says something quite profound: "If I wasn't real, I shouldn't be able to cry!"

When are we more real than when we cry, when the mask of poses and platitudes we display in our make-believe dream world dissolves and a countenance, hurt and tearful, emerges to awaken spontaneous compassion in others? Tears (like the prophet's cry in today's first reading) place a demand on this seemingly mute universe we inhabit—a demand for something more than oblivion, a demand for attention, justice, and love.

Tears declare that if there is a sleeping King or Creator somewhere, he had better wake up and get real and begin to care. But, of course, as Christians we are already convinced there is no sleeping Creator to wake up—but one already quite wide awake, whose constant endeavor has been to make us wake up and become as compassionate and caring (and therefore as real) as God and Christ have ever been.

TWENTY-EIGHTH SNDAY IN ORDINARY TIME

2 Kings 5:14–17

Go Bathe in the Jordan!

Naaman, the wealthy commander of the Syrian army, was offended when the Israelite prophet Elisha prescribed that, in order to cure his leprosy, he simply go bathe in the Jordan River. There were larger and cleaner rivers in his own country, so how dare Elisha suggest the muddy Jordan! Well, maybe the prophet's prescription was intended to do more than cure his leprosy; maybe it was designed to get lofty Namaan down off his high horse, to bring him down to earth.

Naaman's attitude is reflective of an age-old human tendency, namely: to disdain anything that is finite, imperfect, or exhaustible;

to resent the inconvenience of change; to demand a "correct" world as opposed to the mud, blood, sweat, tears, and surprises of the world we actually live in. It's a perfectionism critical even of the face we see in the mirror (we could be so much more handsome or beautiful or forever young). It's a perfectionism that's impatient with delays, with government, with liturgies, or a person's voice or posture; with one's own mistakes and especially those of others. And, of course, it's a perfectionism that's doomed to be forever uncomfortable in a world destined to remain as meandering and muddy and fluid as the Jordan River.

Some people, fully possessed of disdain for this fragile, changeable world, manifest their frustration by way of a hyper-critical attitude. They make it their paid academic or journalistic vocation to complain, to dismantle life or society or human creeds and institutions, to show their inadequacies. To a degree this can be a contribution to society because it's good for us to recognize the limitations and "illusions" of the world we live in. But when such criticism becomes stridently hyper, you have to wonder how much the critic's spleen (instead of his mind and heart) is involved.

Then there is this other type of perfectionist whose disdain for aspects of this world can develop into actual hatred and result in attempts to physically destroy whatever he perceives as imperfect, unclean, too finite and unorthodox to exist. Such is the person who longs for some golden age in opposition to the complex present; who is nostalgic for some ideal society, unblemished in terms of what he deems "correct." The more he finds his ideal contradicted by the "polluted" influences of this current world, the more angry, impersonal, and cold-hearted he becomes—the more he feels righteously called to purge the world of its sins and sinners. Purity becomes his passion, and the annihilation of all that is flawed becomes his relentless ambition. We saw something of that in New York and Washington on September 11, 2001.

Now we ourselves may not suffer from literal leprosy but we do have symptoms of that same disdain or arrogance Naaman manifested when Elisha suggested he immerse himself in the muddy Jordan. We all are inclined to be hypercritical, impatient with things finite and fluid, and unmerciful toward flawed people and institutions. We are all perfectionists, whether it shows itself in sulking or in outright abuse of others.

According to scripture, the only remedy is for us to reverse this deadly tendency and do what Naaman finally did: go bathe in the muddy Jordan, lay aside our often self-serving "standards of perfection," and get to know the infinite depths of every apparently flawed or finite person or phenomenon we meet. Thereby we will emerge from our crotchety self to become like a newborn babe again: eager to experience the mysterious world around us not judgmentally but with new found reverence, with loving curiosity. Go bathe in the Jordan!

TWENTY-NINTH SUNDAY IN ORDINARY TIME

Luke 18:1–8

Pray Always without Becoming Weary

On September 13, 2001, contrary to all expectations, my wife Jane and I took off for Italy as planned. This was but two days after the unspeakable crimes of September 11. I was of two minds after those events: to cancel our trip or to go anyway (if it were possible with the airports shut down). I chose to go, if only to immerse myself in another atmosphere and erase the images of that fateful day.

But after an 11-hour flight on Alitalia from San Francisco and a sojourn in that jewel of a city, Spoleto, in Umbria, the images remained. It was as if I had tried to outrun those clouds of dust that cascaded down Manhattan's streets only to have them catch up to me and engulf me after all. I had thought that the ancient facade of Spoleto's cathedral with its marvelous blue and gold mosaic of

Christ and Mary and Saint John, or its interior frescoes by Filippo
Lippi depicting events in Mary's life, or the civilized panorama
of a medieval city with its narrow streets and crowning citadel
would be powerful enough to purge my memory of the incon-
ceivable evil I had beheld and restore my faith in humanity.

But initially they were of no avail. I would stand there in
the cathedral piazza, enter one church after another, sip coffee from
a terrace where I could take in the beauty of the Ponte delle Torri,
a fourteenth-century bridge of many arches spanning a gorge 240
feet deep, and ask myself: "What relevance do any of these frescoes
and facades, these charming Umbrian towns have in the aftermath
of so violent an event?" September 11's manifestation of human
hatred, intensified by a righteousness bereft of the least compassion,
turned everything beautiful—before my eyes—to ashes.

And then I realized that I was letting the toxicity of that
event infiltrate my very heart and mind, a toxicity that would render
me one more casualty. And it was fright over such a consequence
that awoke me, possibly for the first time in my life, to the fact that
faith is indeed a feeble thing if all it amounts to is a passive inheri-
tance, a habit, a mere reflex as involuntary as breathing. It hit me
that faith must be a willful thing possessed of the defiance exhibited
by the woman in today's parable. True faith is no mere "maybe"
to be easily shaken by contradictions no matter how terrible. True
faith amounts to an invincible "Yes!" to life rendered only the more
vigorous by any subtle or outrageous coercion to despair.

And so I resolved that henceforth I would target not the
airfields or bunkers of some political landscape but the very
landscape of my heart, to nip in the bud my least tendency to sneer,
to criticize other people, to damn inconvenience, to doubt my own
worth, to ridicule the politically or aesthetically "incorrect"—in
a word, to purge my own heart of those sour, resentful, negative
tendencies that throughout humanity's history have been the seed-
bed out of which the chilling hatred we saw on that September 11
eventually emerges.

And I resolved to cherish every apple I see (be it bruised or not), every park and tree (even the unwelcome eucalyptus), every checkout person or banker I meet, every Cal Trans worker sweating over the asphalt, every human artifact (be it a billboard or a cathedral or a cheap vase tucked in the corner of a second-hand store window)—in other words, anything that testifies to humanity's capacity to create, however modestly, rather than destroy a world.

THIRTIETH SUNDAY IN ORDINARY TIME

Sirach 35:12–14, 16–18, Emily Dickinson, Matthew Arnold, W.B. Yeats

The Prayer of the Lowly Pierces the Clouds

Despondency crept into the poetry of our culture around the mid 1800s. You find it even in the verse of Emily Dickinson who lived in so placid a town as Amherst, Massachusetts. Finding little comfort in the homilies of her Puritan heritage, she sensed an emptiness to life that she referred to as "the Blank" and expressed at times in poems like this:

> After great pain, a formal feeling comes—
> The Nerves sit ceremonious, like Tombs—
> The stiff Heart questions was it He, that bore,
> And Yesterday, or Centuries before?
>
> The Feet, mechanical, go round . . .
> A Wooden way
> Regardless grown . . .
>
> This is the Hour of Lead—
> Remembered, if outlived,

As Freezing persons, recollect the Snow—
First—Chill—then Stupor—then the letting go—[50]

Her mood was not unlike that of Matthew Arnold, who put his finger on the likely cause of so much despondency in his famous poem "Dover Beach," namely our transition from an age of faith into an era of secular doubt and skepticism:

> The Sea of Faith
> Was once, too, at the full, and round earth's shore
> Lay like the folds of a bright girdle furled.
> But now I only hear
> Its melancholy, long, withdrawing roar,
> Retreating, to the breath
> Of the night wind, down the vast edges near
> And naked shingles of the world. . . .
> And we are here as on a darkling plain
> Swept with confused alarms of struggle and flight
> Where ignorant armies clash by night.[51]

Nor did the arrival of the 1900s relieve such despondency. The continual warfare of the twentieth century, the insoluble hatreds prevailing in so many parts of the world were enough to make people wonder if there really was a God, whether we were not simply adrift in a vacant universe. William Butler Yeats, way back in 1921, found little solace in the Christian story of Christmas. He anticipated the birth of something else:

> Surely the Second Coming is at hand.
> . . . somewhere in sands of the desert
> A shape with lion body and the head of a man,
> A gaze bland and pitiless as the sun,
> Is moving its slow thighs . . .

And what rough beast, its hour come round at last,
Slouches toward Bethlehem to be born?[52]

Bereft of their ancestral faith, confronted by a universe that baffles them, such poets experience a profound agony—an agony perhaps even we believers can appreciate as we ourselves are shaken by the craziness of recent events. But can even the secular poet remain completely despondent? May not vestiges of his abandoned faith still move him to see even in the vacancy around him the possibility of a new revelation, the ultimate victory of all that is benign and constructive in human nature?

Though Yeats died despondent, he still saw signs of hope. He lived for a time (as Seamus Heaney reminds us in his Nobel Laureate lecture of 1995) in one of those old round towers in Ireland and noticed one day, stuck in the crevice of the wall, the empty nest of a starling (which in Ireland they sometimes call a stare). In it some bees had made a hive, buzzing with life, laced with honey. The empty nest seemed to him a symbol of this empty modern world of ours but the hive a signal of hope, and so he wrote a poem called "The Stare's Nest by My Window" that really amounts to a secular prayer, which I suggest in these sad times we make our own. It goes like this:

> The bees build in the crevices
> Of loosening masonry . . .
> My wall is loosening; honey-bees,
> Come build in the empty house of the stare.
>
> We are closed in, and the key is turned
> On our uncertainty; somewhere
> A man is killed, or a house burned,
> Yet no clear fact to be discerned:
> Come build in the empty house of the stare. . . .

We had fed the heart on fantasies,
The heart's grown brutal from the fare;
More substance in our enmities
Than in our love; O honey bees,
Come build in the empty house of the stare.[53]

THIRTY-FIRST SUNDAY IN ORDINARY TIME

Luke 19:1–10, Nathaniel Hawthorne

The Big Parade

Clifford Pyncheon (in *The House of the Seven Gables*[54]) had just been released from prison for a crime he did not commit. He had entered as a young man. Gray, hardly able to put one foot before the other, he returned to his sister Hepzibah's home. To his young cousin Phoebe "the expression on his countenance . . . seemed to waver and glimmer, and nearly die away . . . like a flame we see twinkling among half-extinguished embers." When introduced to Phoebe he could not recall who she was.

All he wanted to do now was confine himself to an upstairs room and fade away. But ever so lightly the musical airs sung by Phoebe from downstairs would transfigure his face with pleasure. He became less despondent. There was something so real about her, he began to recover his trust—at least of his environment within the walls of Hepzibah's house. As for the world outside, he could still only view it with dismay and repugnance from an arched upstairs window.

Then one day the banners, drums, fifes, and cymbals of a parade swept past the house, "a mighty river of life, massive in its tide . . . calling to the kindred depth within him. . . . He shuddered; he grew pale, he threw an appealing look at Hepzibah and Phoebe, who were with him at the window." And then, "with tremulous limbs, he started up, set his foot on the window sill, and, in an instant more, would have been on the unguarded balcony. . . . Had Clifford attained the balcony, he would probably have leaped into the street; but whether impelled by the species of terror, that sometimes urges its victim over the very precipice he shrinks from, or by a natural magnetism, tending towards the great centre of humanity—it were not easy to decide." Phoebe and Hepzibah had to restrain him. His sister cried out, "Clifford, Clifford, are you crazy?" to which Clifford replied, "I hardly know, Hepzibah! . . . but had I taken that plunge, and survived it, methinks it would have made me another man!"

That's precisely what Clifford needed to do: lay aside the bitterness and self-pity that kept him still spiritually a prisoner despite his physical release and join that parade, which to my mind is nothing less than a metaphor of that grand parade of salvation history that began with God's call to Abraham, picked up momentum under Moses, and in today's gospel is led with quickening pace by Jesus himself through the streets of Jericho, where we come across another fellow named Zacchaeus, who doesn't want to be left behind.

Zacchaeus was also a person who had chosen to isolate himself from people around him in order to pursue his own self-interest at their expense. The price he had to pay was loneliness, the loss of his humanity. And now here comes this parade! There was something about it and especially its drum major Jesus, that was so alive with joy and solidarity; he simply had to become a part of it. But how? He was so stunted! But he knew a lot about upward mobility! So, climbing a tree, he diverted Jesus' parade right through his domicile, where he demonstrated a new found wholesomeness four times over and won Jesus' declaration that he was indeed eligible to fall in line with Abraham and become a genuine human being after all.

Where do you stand in relation to Hawthorne's Clifford or Luke's Zacchaeus? Have you been traumatized into a state of inertia or has preoccupation with business left you feeling—even opulently—lost in space and time? There is a eucharistic parade that passes through your neighborhood every Sunday, led by Christ and made up of people trying to be people. Don't let it pass you by.

THIRTY-SECOND SUNDAY IN ORDINARY TIME

Luke 20:27–38, Edgar Allan Poe

Close But No Cigar

In his short story "The Purloined Letter," Edgar Allan Poe's main character, Monsieur Dupin, tells of a game people used to play with a map. Let's say it was a map of France that showed and named its counties, cities, towns, and villages in large or small letters. The rules of the game were simple. One player would select a locality's name and challenge the other players to guess what it was. Now normally a novice at the game might select one of the tinier localities bearing one of the tinier, less apparent names. But the really shrewd player would choose the name of FRANCE itself, because, being printed in the largest letters and spaced across the whole map, it was very likely to be overlooked by everybody—"by dint of its being excessively obvious."

You could say that is the very reason the religious leaders of Jesus' time overlooked him entirely. Like the usual player of Dupin's game, they, too, had this tendency to study only fine print, assuming that was where they might find the answer to the quiz of human existence. And all the while Jesus walked among them like the name of FRANCE written spaciously across the whole landscape of the times in which they lived.

By that I mean smallness was their preference. Their concept of God had become petty. They saw him merely as the Chief
Justice of the Cosmic Supreme Court, author of a million petty ways
of doing things, the source of minute rules covering everything from
Sabbath behavior and hygiene to the limited options open to child-
less widows. They saw him as narrowly partial to his chosen people
and disdainful of Samaritans, Syrians, prostitutes, publicans, and
"different" people in general. (All of which makes one suspect that
this aloof, biased, and irritable God was more a reflection of themselves than the original and intimate God of the Bible who walked
with Adam in the cool of the evening and dined in triplicate with
ancient Abraham outside his shepherd's tent.)

And since Jesus didn't fall within their narrow concept of
God and their God's way of doing things, they ultimately wrote him
off. Oh yes, when he first came on the scene valuing people more
than rubrics, saying things like the Sabbath was made for people and
not people for the Sabbath; when he did not hesitate to dine with
a public sinner or to allow himself to be touched by a prostitute;
when he began to forgive people's sins as though it was the easiest
thing in the world to do, they did become curious and concerned.
They sent delegations to size him up, to match him against the standards of the ominous God they worshipped and found him totally
out of sync. They couldn't contain him within the old wine skins
they had brought along. His responses to their three dimensional
questions had a strange, four dimensional ring to them. So they
turned away to continue their tedious search for the answers to life
amid the footnotes of their tired tradition.

And yet there was Jesus in CAPITAL LETTERS, as large
as life itself, as large as true God must be: caring, forgiving, healing,
uttering parables loaded with grace, ready to lay down his life
a thousand times over for everyone and anyone. Right there among
them was the incarnation of the only God worth believing in,
a Creator of unrelenting understanding and compassion.

You know the old saying about a person's not being able to see the forest for the trees. Therein lies a warning to all of us. Never allow yourself to miss the obvious truth by too much analysis. Our creed is a simple one: God is LOVE and those who abide in LOVE abide in God and God in them!

THIRTY-THIRD SUNDAY IN ORDINARY TIME

Malachi 3:19–20a, Luke 21:5–19, Charles Dickens

Something Will Turn Up

My favorite character in *David Copperfield*[55] is Mr. Wilkins Micawber. In the old film version of the book, Micawber's part was played by W. C. Fields (if anyone remembers him). Micawber was an enterprising man. He undertook business ventures in coal and corn, which never paid off. Or he would rent a house to take in boarders, only to find himself, his family and boarders evicted because he had fallen behind in the rent.

Creditors like the milkman and shoemaker used to post themselves outside his house at seven o'clock in the morning to catch him before he went out. But they never could, because at such times he would hide in the shadows of an upstairs room until they left. Actually, his usual way of meeting debt was to write an I.O.U. and deliver it in such a sincere and solemn manner that the recipient almost felt he had been paid.

Given his inability ever to make ends meet, the economic status of his large family was always precarious and this would deeply depress the man. But no matter how depressed he was for the moment, he was at heart an optimist, ever expectant. As David Copperfield notes upon first meeting the man: "I have known him to come home to supper with a flood of tears and a declaration that nothing was now left but a jail; and go to bed making a calculation of the expense of putting a bow-window in the house, 'in case anything turned up.' "

Indeed, that phrase "in case anything turned up" or some variation of it was Micawber's favorite. For example, when considering emigrating to Australia, he consoles his wife with his conviction that under existing impecunious circumstances, Australia is "the land, the only land, for myself and my family; and that something of an extraordinary nature will turn up on that shore."

And so what happens in the course of the novel? We meet that serpentine villain, Uriah Heep, a symbol of hypocrisy and greed if there ever was one, who has become administrator of the business of Mr. Wickfield, the future father-in-law of David Copperfield. While feigning humility, Heep slowly takes advantage of Mr. Wickfield's ineptitude until he controls the firm and aspires to marry Wickfield's daughter Agnes. And whom should Uriah Heep hire as his clerk but Mr. Micawber, who over time observes Heep's trickery, discovers Heep's private notebook that records Heep's false accounting, and exposes the man, redeeming the happiness of all the major characters in the novel!

So for all his expectation that something will turn up, who is it that finally turns up but Mr. Micawber himself! And isn't there a lesson in that turn of events for us? We live expectantly. We listen to scripture readings about the second coming of Christ. Some people go so far as to predict its date in hopes that the injustice of this world might soon be exposed and give way to a kingdom more humane and beautiful. And yet things remain the same, or worse. But why? Because perhaps in God's subtle plan of things, Jesus and his reign are not destined simply to arrive on some particular future date, but in each of us hour after hour, day after day, in so far as each of us manifests something of Christ's grace and healing power in our world.

In other words, even as we live ever expectant of something turning up, maybe it's really time for each of us to "turn up" in a redemptive way as Micawber did, much to his own surprise.

THIRTY-THIRD SUNDAY IN ORDINARY TIME
TOPICAL: THE INCREMENTAL NATURE OF CHRIST'S SECOND COMING

Charles Dickens

Gabriel's Horn

I think I first heard Gabriel's trumpet ever so faintly when I was about seven years old. I lived at the time in a depression-struck working class neighborhood of Philadelphia. My father was becoming quietly desperate by almost continual unemployment. My mother was becoming correspondingly cautious and disenchanted with domestic life. In other words, the house was tense. And so were the streets. Fist fights were almost daily encouraged among boys my age and older as part of an accepted process whereby we developed into "real men."

Then one day at a gathering of relatives someone handed me a small book titled *Lives of the Saints.* I opened it to find a picture of Saint James on one page and an account of his life on the other. There he was with brown beard, blue eyes, wearing a blue robe with brown cloak, holding a staff, feet shod with sandals. And there were Saints Jude, John, Paul, Cecilia, Agnes, and Francis, with ultra pink faces and pink feet, some looking quite sober, others smiling, but all with a far away look in their eyes. And I thought, "These are friends. There's something about them that's different, something true. They see something I don't see and want to see."

Gabriel's trumpet sounded again for me whenever I entered Saint Ludwig's Church in that old neighborhood. Outside the church were blocks upon blocks of two storied row houses punctuated by high factories and warehouses as far as the eye could see. It was a world similar to Coketown in Dickens's novel *Hard Times:*[56] "a town of machinery and tall chimneys, out of which interminable serpents of smoke trailed . . . and where what you couldn't state in figures, or show to be purchasable in the cheapest market and saleable in the dearest, was not, and never should be, world without end, Amen."

Yet on the other side of the oak doors of Saint Ludwig's there lay another reality. There I came upon the same placid saints of my book, now distributed throughout the place on pedestals from which they looked down on me with the same summoning eyes. There also I found gospel stories enacted all around me in windows of blue and red and yellow: frightened disciples in a storm tossed boat and Jesus standing in their midst about to calm the sea, little children gathering around the knees of Jesus while disciples tried to turn them away, Jesus summoning a pallid Lazarus out of his tomb while friends looked on amazed. All bathed me in their light. There was something wonderful about this place. It seemed an antechamber to a civilization more real, more desirable than Coketown.

Later on I entered a high school run by the Christian Brothers. These men were tough. They would knock you for a loop on the football field during intramural games. But there was also something different about them. They seemed motivated by something more sublime than self-preservation—something expressed in the motto inscribed in large golden letters around the ceiling of their baroque chapel. It was a line from the prophet Daniel. The day I first looked up and noticed it Gabriel's horn sounded again for me. It read, "Those who instruct many unto justice shall shine as stars for all eternity." Whatever it meant, the image made a permanent impression on me: to shine like a star for all eternity.

We associate Gabriel's trumpet with the end of the world. But as you can see, worlds end everyday: every time we are inspired to question the limitations of the common sense world around us, every time we begin to believe there is more to life than achieving material security, every time we become convinced that our primary reason for existing is to become a saint, that is, a big-hearted, hopeful, irrepressibly forgiving and sociable human being—in other words, a poet in the deepest sense of the word. Whenever that happens, the immature world around us begins to crumble ever so much and Jesus (representing an ultimately humane humanity) begins to appear ever so faintly on the horizon. The end of the world is not something we wait for. It's something that happens to us, every time we hear Gabriel blow his horn.

THE COMMEMORATION
OF ALL THE FAITHFUL DEPARTED

1 Corinthians 15:51–57, Emily Dickinson, James Joyce

She Went As Quiet As the Dew

> She went as quiet as the Dew
> From an Accustomed flower.
> Not like the Dew, did she return
> At the Accustomed hour![57]

I was curious that I felt so little emotions as I knelt three weeks ago in a front pew, close to my mother's casket, while a strange priest recited the prayers of her funeral Mass. Actually I felt numb, too weary to think or say anything by way of a eulogy, to fabricate pleasant thoughts or wade through memories, or in any way fill the void while my own soul felt so empty.

But isn't that the way it is with death? Its initial impact seems to bring us up short, to cancel all thought of business as usual. Suddenly the absolute absence of someone we took for granted makes us absentminded, wondering why, who's next, and what it's all about. Here was a life worthy of a novel: a sad-faced three-year-old girl in a 1912 photo; a 1920s flapper, complete with Louise Brooks hair style; a waitress at Abe's Oyster House, whose tips got us through the Depression; then playing Rosie the Riveter circa 1943; still bowling while practically blind in her eighties; and then erased from the chalkboard of human history. It makes one pause and wonder.

"Wonder about what?" says the cynic within my breast. "What did you expect? Oblivion awaits us all. We'll no more be remembered within this silent universe than last week's headlines." Or to allow that more classic materialist Buck Mulligan (the swaggering medical intern in James Joyce's novel *Ulysses*) to express it in his terms: "And what is death . . . your mother's or yours or my own? You saw only your mother die. I see them pop off every day in the Mater and Richmond and cut up into tripes in the dissecting-room. It's a beastly thing and nothing else . . . Her cerebral lobes are not functioning. She calls doctor sir Peter Teazle and picks buttercups off the quilt. Humour her till it's over."[58]

Yet while I kneel there gazing unseeing at the sanctuary floor, the celebrant's voice begins to infiltrate my benumbed brain. His words become clearer. "Now I am going to tell you a mystery," he says. "In an instant, in the twinkling of an eye, at the sound of the last trumpet . . . the dead will be raised incorruptible, and we shall be changed. Then the saying of Scripture will be fulfilled: Death is swallowed up in victory." And again: "Lord of mercy, may our sister Mary, whom you called your daughter on earth, enter the kingdom of peace and light where your saints live in glory."

And I think to myself: Here is the great gift of my Catholic tradition, this defiance, this refusal to remain numb in the face of death, this power of the imagination to envision realities that lie beyond the evidence of our senses. We take events like birth, marriage, sickness, and death, and turn them into sacramental moments, embroidering them with ritual and poetry and prayers that reveal them to be so much more than ultimately meaningless biological or physical or economic phenomena.

And I say, "Yes, this and not the fatalism of Mulligan is what speaks to my heart and therefore tells me the whole truth and nothing short of the truth!" And in my heart I thank the celebrant and the lady in the choir and the people on their knees around me who testify to that traditional vision, and I turn to look at my mother's casket next to me and remember another fragment of verse of that New England saint, Emily Dickinson:

> A Coffin—is a small Domain
> Yet able to contain
> A Citizen of Paradise
> In its diminished Plane.
>
> A Grave—is a restricted Breadth—
> Yet ampler than the Sun—
> And all the Seas He populates
> And Lands He looks upon
>
> To Him who on its small Repose
> Bestows a single Friend—
> Circumference without Relief—
> Or Estimate—or End—[59]

LAST SUNDAY IN ORDINARY TIME
OUR LORD JESUS CHRIST THE KING

Colossians 1:12–20, Isak Dinesen

He Delivered Us from Darkness and Transferred Us to the Kingdom of His Beloved Son

"Madame, we who are by birth the grandees of the King, and hereditary office-holders of his court, and who have the code of *Le Grand Monarque* in our veins . . . must keep up his glory. For the people must not doubt the greatness of the King . . . and the responsibility for keeping up their faith rests upon you and me, Madame."[60]

Cardinal Hamilcar addresses these words to the aging Miss Nat-og-Dag in Isak Dinesen's tale "The Deluge at Norderney." He reminds her that both he and she are aristocrats and as such must behave with a largesse and courage beyond the level of ordinary folk. He does so because at that moment both are stranded in the loft of a sinking barn. A storm out of the North Sea had broken through the dikes of Norderney and flooded the countryside, and although the Cardinal and Miss Nat-og-Dag were among the last to be rescued, they gave up their place in the boat to some farm people who had been trapped in the loft. True, the boatmen had promised to return for them the following morning, but both knew that the barn would sink before then and so they quietly, proudly awaited their fate, conversing the night away. Why? Because they were aristocrats, educated from infancy to the concept of *noblesse oblige.* Plebeians might scramble to save their own skins but not people aware of their aristocratic responsibility to display benevolent behavior.

Isak Dinesen makes this point often in her stories. She was distressed with our modern era. Yes, we have been blessed by technological progress. Life has become comfortable. Death and disease have taken a low profile. Our stores are stocked with more than we'll ever need. But for all this material progress, we seem to have become increasingly selfish, boorish, and intolerant of any demands on us. For example, what's that old refrain we hear whenever somebody proposes helping the homeless? "Not in my backyard!"

To Isak Dinesen this is a petty bourgeois way of thinking, an attitude characteristic of the vacationers who thronged the resorts around Norderney. In pre-modern times their ancestors would not have dared approach the coast, because the sea was seen as simply raw nature, full of awesome creatures, a thing to be respected and revered. But for the present vacationers, technology had long since tamed nature to the point where they had made of it another toy. They built casinos, waded under parasols by the water's edge, put up their easels near a quaint old shipwreck (the relic of some for-gotten horror).

Until Isak Dinesen inserted into her story a sudden storm (the worst in a hundred years) that shattered all their illusions about the security of their fragile resort and sent them scurrying inland in whatever vehicle was available—in keeping with the pre-vailing philosophy of a self-indulgent age: every man for himself, survival of the fittest, and fastest out of here! Everyone except for our Cardinal and Miss Nat-og-Dag, relics of a more heroic era. They are people educated to see in difficulties a chance to show the stuff they were made of—to make of death itself a magnanimous gesture in the manner of Jesus Christ.

I'm sure it was Jesus (and not Louis XIV) whom Isak Dinesen had in mind when the Cardinal in her story utters the quotation at the top of this essay. And I'm wondering if Pope Pius XI didn't share something of the mind of Isak Dinesen when he instituted this feast of Christ the King to remind us that, having been baptized in the royal blood of Jesus, we are to be no longer plebeian in attitude but are to behave always as befits the grandees of a *Grand Monarque*.

MEMORIAL DAY

Thomas Helm

Meditations from a Life Raft

Prior to a flight last month, I surveyed the airport's paperback bookshelves. I wasn't too hopeful because nowadays newsstands seem to offer little you can sink your teeth into. But just before turning away I spotted Thomas Helm's account of the sinking of the U.S.S. *Indianapolis* in World War II, titled *Ordeal by Sea.*[61] Do you know about the *Indianapolis?* It was July of 1945. The war in the Pacific would be over in two weeks. But that was not foreseen by the cruiser's 1,196 officers and men who, after their unescorted departure from the island of Tinian en route to the Philippines, were either on watch or trying to sleep when at one minute after midnight on July 30 two torpedoes struck, sinking the ship in less than twenty minutes. For five days and nights the survivors floated in life jackets and rafts over a 10-mile stretch of the ocean without water or food, subject to frequent shark attacks—until on the fifth day only 317 were left.

Besides the agony of their ordeal, what especially impressed me were the fantasies that set in among the men. One thought the ship was only twenty feet below and that the cooks were still in the galley dishing out meals. Another thought he felt a fresh water river welling up from the bottom of the ocean. Others believed an island was only thirty miles away and kept paddling against the wind toward a vision of its sun drenched beach and coconut palms. I was struck by how active faith and hope become in situations of distress. These men were now reaching out with hyperactive imaginations in every direction to anticipate a happy ending to their plight.

And I thought: what a perfect metaphor of our own collective situation on this tiny globe (which is little more than a life raft adrift within a vast ocean of space) subject as we are, if not to frequent shark attacks, then to disease, war, accident, confusion. And what have we humans been doing down through the ages but envisioning scenarios of rescue. I mean, what are the works of Homer or Chaucer or Dickens or Flannery O'Connor or so many poets but aspirations of a positive outcome to our mortal existence? And what, especially, is the Bible but a heritage of creative faith telling us, by way of the story of Noah and the Exodus and Jonah and Christ's resurrection that, far from our being hopelessly lost in time and space, we are enveloped by grace and that ultimately Christ will come walking toward us upon the water?

Of course, many practical people consider our biblical interpretation of life of no scientific validity, no more than a hallucination. But such nihilists would not be as welcome at later reunions of the *Indianapolis* survivors as was Lieutenant Wilbur Gwinn, the pilot who finally spotted them and initiated their rescue. On one of these occasions Lieutenant Gwinn said: "Some of my reflections have been so startling as to make me think of miracles. Sometimes I believe we are living in a world of miracles . . . What were the chances you would be found? . . . What were the chances that Wilbur Gwinn would fly a course that would take him directly over you? . . . The odds . . . were one in a million. . . . Somehow he was chosen as the instrument to overcome these astronomical odds."

Of course, one may ask, "What about the other 879 whom Gwinn came too late to save?" But to ask that is to underestimate the full scope of Christian faith and hope as expressed, for example, in the closing verses of the book of Revelation: "Then I saw the heavens opened and . . . a great white throne and one who sat upon it from whose face heaven and earth took flight . . . and the sea gave up its dead . . . And I saw a new heaven and a new earth for the prior heaven and prior earth had passed away—and there was no more sea" (Revelation 19:11—21:1, author's translation).

FOURTH OF JULY

Nathaniel Hawthorne

Revolution

"Shall we never, never get rid of this Past," cried Holgrave. "It lies upon the Present like a giant's dead body! In fact, the case is just as if a young giant were compelled to waste all his strength in carrying about the corpse of the old giant, his grandfather, who died a long while ago, and only needs to be decently buried. Just think a moment; and it will startle you to see what slaves we are to bygone times."[62]

Holgrave, a character in Hawthorne's novel *The House of the Seven Gables*, strongly believed in progress and the primacy of reason over the old myths that once beclouded people's minds. He believed in the freedom to cast off "the moss-grown and rotten past and lifeless institutions" and begin everything anew. He favored independence, ambition—physical, mental and professional mobility. He himself had been a schoolmaster, salesman, editor, dentist, sailor, and lecturer, and had recently taken up a newfangled thing called photography. He despised settling down so much that he believed no public building should be made of stone or brick (not even the U.S. Capitol). "It were better," he said, "that they should crumble into ruin, once in twenty years . . . as a hint to the people to examine into and reform the institutions they symbolize." As for private dwellings, they should be no more durable than a bird's nest, to be left behind while we move on to what is fashionable next year.

Holgrave embodied for Hawthorne all the values of the American Revolution, which we celebrate this weekend—values that certainly permeated my consciousness, growing up as I did in the Cradle of Liberty otherwise known as Philadelphia.

Boston might boast of Paul Revere, the Old North Church, its famous Tea Party, Lexington, Concord, and Bunker Hill, but we natives of the City of Brotherly Love had as much and more to be provincially proud of: Independence Hall, the Betsy Ross House, the Liberty Bell, the Declaration, the Constitution, Valley Forge, and the Battle of Brandywine. We could match the Boston Massacre with the Paoli Massacre. I used to play out on the lawn of Strawberry Mansion where that traitor Benedict Arnold once courted Peggy Shippen. My school stood near the Chew House, still marked by the canister of the Battle of Germantown. My Boy Scout camp lay a mile or so above the spot where Washington crossed the Delaware. The American Revolution was in the very air we breathed. You could say the 1700s were still a current event.

But we were also Catholic and, much as the good nuns impressed on us the Catholic contribution to the Revolution (Commodore John Barry, signer Charles Carroll, Pulaski, Kosciusko, Lafayette, and all the French soldiers who made the difference at Yorktown), they also admonished us not to despise the past. They reminded us that the world didn't begin in 1776, that we indeed had a vital past that went all the way back to Abraham—a heritage that valued revolutionary freedom but also faith, compassion, solidarity, and Christic self-sacrifice as the qualities upon which a truly sane commonwealth must be built.

In other words, as Catholic Americans we were educated to be not so iconoclastic (or should I say modern or postmodern?) as Holgrave about ancient, deeper values. We were educated to be more like Hawthorne's other character Phoebe who taught Holgrave to allow his heart and a bit of common sense to influence his head. In the end we find him bartering his once haughty, revolutionary faith for a far humbler one "in discerning that man's best-directed effort accomplishes a kind of dream, while God is the sole worker of realities."

LABOR DAY

Dylan Thomas

Labor Day is more like Memorial Day for me. It reminds me of all who died in more ways than one during the Great Depression of the 1930s. It brings back memories of my father, who was a laboring man, who lifted things, climbed ladders, and worked with his hands. He started as a roofer in his mid-teens. I have a photograph of him taken during a lunch break on a Philadelphia rooftop with several other grimy looking fellows, all wearing those caps that were the fashion of the working class. You can almost smell the tar.

By the time he was twenty he had become an excellent sheet metal man, making rain gutters, vents, panels, things that required even artistic skill. And everyday from 1926 until 1947 he recorded in a notebook his worksite, hours and incidental costs.

Here's a sample of what he wrote.

> 1926: Sept. 9, Tasker St., Spout, 8 hours, fare 13 cents . . .
> Sept. 11, 3rd and Jefferson, Skylight, 10 hours, fare 9 cents . . .
> Oct. 15, Rain . . .
>
> 1927: Jan. 7, Villanova, Repair, 8 hours, phone 5 cents . . .
> Jan. 8, Snow . . .
> Feb. 9, Married Mary . . .
>
> 1928: Jan. 20, 34th and Spruce, 8 hours . . .
> Jan. 21, Baby Born, 12:45 AM . . .
> Jan. 22, 34th and Spruce, 8 hours, fare 10 cents.

Though interspersed with brief personal notes, it was on the whole a record of hard work and (after 1929) of months when he faithfully recorded: "No work, No work, No work." A record, too, of weekly salaries of $13.00 until the WPA hired him in the late 1930s to work at the Navy Yard for an incredible $42.00 every two weeks!

It's not that he was without ambition. Entering the Roaring Twenties, he shared the hopes of his generation. He dreamed of suburban happiness. He crooned songs about "a smiling face, a fire place, a cozy room; a place to nestle in where the roses bloom." He danced the Charleston. But by 1943, his youth was somehow gone. Shamed during the Depression years by a foreclosure on his first home, forced to crowd his family into his mother's house, forced for a time to go on Relief, he had begun to drink in a counterproductive effort to quell his frustration.

By that time I was long gone! By the age of 15, I had developed a distaste for twentieth-century economics and went off to live in the thirteenth century of *Il Poverello:* I entered a Franciscan monastery. I never realized how much that added to his sense of despair because I never felt we had any real relationship. I had felt myself to be a mere inhabitant of his household, a bemused, often frightened observer of his decline and fall. I found out later he wept often over the emptiness of my room.

He lies buried today in the cemetery of Mother of Sorrows parish in Philadelphia. How appropriate a name, for the spires of Mother of Sorrows now look down upon a sprawling African American ghetto where young men in their struggle to survive feel the same confusion and rage my father felt—a rage God himself must share as he beholds so many millions of his children laboring simply to survive in a world rich enough to support and promote the human potential of us all.

I used to fear your rage, my father. I understand it now, and make my own the dirge Dylan Thomas wept over his father:

> Do not go gentle into that good night,
> Old age should burn and rave at close of day;
> Rage, rage against the dying of the light. . . .

And you, my father, there on the sad height,

Curse, bless, me now with your fierce tears, I pray.

Do not go gentle into that good night.

Rage, rage against the dying of the light.[63]

Endnotes

1. F. Scott Fitzgerald, *The Great Gatsby* (Bantam Books edition, 1974), p. 186.

2. Herman Melville, *Moby Dick* (New York: Random House edition, 1930), pp. 757–762.

3. Charles Dickens, "A Christmas Carol" in *Christmas Books* (New York: Charles Scribners Sons, 1897), pp. 91–92.

4. John Galsworthy, *The Forsyte Saga* (New York: Simon and Schuster, Inc., 2002). All quotations are from this edition.

5. "You Can Tell The World" as recorded by Simon and Garfunkel, Label: Columbia, (LP CS 9049, CD CK 9049, CD CBS 63370) Words and Music: B. Gibson, B. Camp; 1961 Melody Trails, Inc., New York, New York.

6. Charles Dickens, "A Christmas Carol" in *Christmas Books* (New York: Charles Scribners Sons, 1897). All quotations are from this edition.

7. Willa Cather, *My Ántonia* (Boston: Houghton Mifflin, 1954). All quotations are from this edition.

8. Mark Twain, *The Adventures of Huckleberry Finn* (New York: The Modern Library edition, 1993), p. 124. All quotations are from this edition.

9. Amy Witting, "A Curse on Herod" in *Chapters Into Verse: A Selection of Poetry in English Inspired by the Bible,* ed. Robert Atwan and Laurance Wieder (New York: Oxford University Press, 2000), p. 272.

10. Richard Brautigan, "My Catfish Friend" in *The Pill versus The Springhill Mine Disaster,* (New York: Dell Publishing Company, Inc., A Delta Book, 1968), p. 97.

11. Emily Dickinson, *The Complete Poems of Emily Dickinson,* ed. Thomas H. Johnson (Boston: Little, Brown and Company, 1960). All of Emily Dickinson's poems cited here are from this edition.

12. Mark Twain, *The Adventures of Huckleberry Finn* (New York: Modern Library edition, 1993), pp. 92–95.

13. Willa Cather, *My Ántonia* (Boston: Houghton Mifflin Company, 1954), pp. 352–353.

14. Charles Dickens, *A Tale of Two Cities* (London and New York: Penguin Books, 1988). All quotations are from this edition.

15. Percy Bysshe Shelley, "Hymn to Intellectual Beauty" in *Complete Works of John Keats and Percy Bysshe Shelley* (New York: Random House, The Modern Library), p. 115.

16. Frances Burnett, *The Secret Garden* (New York: Harper Collins). All quotations are from this edition.

17. Ernest Hemingway, *A Farewell to Arms* (New York: Simon and Schuster, Scribner Paperback Fiction, 1995). All quotations are from this edition.

18. Kathy Evans, "Today in Juvy," *americas review* #12, P.O. Box 7681 Berkeley, California, 94707, pp. 33–34.

19. Marcel Proust, *In Search of Lost Time,* vol. 5, trans. C.K. Moncrieff and Terence Kilmartin (New York: Random House, The Modern Library edition, 1989). All quotations are from this edition.

20. Ranier Maria Rilke, "Death Experienced" in *New Poems 1907,* trans. Edward Snow (New York: North Point Press, Farrar, Strauss and Giroux, 1994), p. 111.

21. Robert Service, "The Quest" in *Collected Poems of Robert Service* (New York: Dodd, Mead and Company, 1961), p. 538.

22. Thomas Traherne, "Dumnesse" in *The Poetical Books of Thomas Traherne,* ed. Gladys I. Wade (New York: Cooper Square Publishers, Inc., 1965), p. 23.

23. John Keats, "On First Looking Into Chapman's Homer," *The Complete Works of John Keats and Percy Bysshe Shelley* (New York: Random House, The Modern Library), p. 32.

24. Marcel Proust, *In Search of Lost Time,* vol. 2, trans. C. K. Scott Moncrieff and Terence Kilmartin (New York: Random House, Modern Library edition, 1998). All quotations are from this edition.

25. Mark Twain, *The Adventures of Huckleberry Finn* (New York: The Modern Library edition, 1993) pp. 346–348.

26. Mark Twain, *The Adventures of Tom Sawyer* (Chicago: A World Library Limited edition, Field Enterprises Educational Corporation, 1975). All quotations are from this edition.

27. *The Collected Writings of Walt Whitman,* ed. Gay Wilson Allen and Sculley Bradley (New York: New York University Press, 1965).

28. Michael Chabon, *The Amazing Adventures of Kavalier and Clay* (New York: Random House, Inc., 2000). All quotations are from this edition.

29. John O'Hara, "Bread Alone" in *Selected Short Stories of John O'Hara* (New York: Random House, The Modern Library edition, 1956), pp. 100–105.

30. George Eliot, *Middlemarch,* edit. W. J. Harvey (Harmondsworth:The Penguin Edition English Library, 1965).

31. Victor Hugo, *Les Misérables,* trans. Norman Denny (London/New York: Penguin Books, 1982). All quotations are from this edition.

32. "Auguries of Innocence" in *The Complete Poetry and Selected Prose of John Donne and The Complete Poetry of William Blake* (New York: Random House, The Modern Library, 1941), p. 597.

33. e. e. cummings, *100 Selected Poems* (New York: Grove Weidenfield, a division of Grove Press, Inc., 1959), p. 114.

34. Willa Cather, *O Pioneers!* (Pleasantville, New York: The Reader's Digest Association, Inc., 1990). All quotations are from this edition.

35. Gerald Vann, OP, *The Paradise Tree* (New York: Sheed and Ward, 1959).

36. Flannery O'Connor, "Parker's Back" in *Wise Blood, The Violent Bear It Away, The Complete Stories* (New York: Quality Paperback Book Club, 1992), pp. 510–530. All quotations are from this edition.

37. Nathaniel Hawthorne, *The House of Seven Gables* (New York: The Library of America, Literary Classics of the United States, Inc., 1983). All quotations are from this edition.

38. "Holy Sonnets" in *The Golden Hind: An Anthology of Elizabethan Prose and Poetry,* revised edition (New York: W. W. Norton and Company, Inc., 1956), p. 828.

39. Ranier Maria Rilke, "The Man Watching" in *News of the Universe: Poems of Twofold Consciousness,* ed. Robert Bly (New York: Sierra Club Books, 1980), pp. 121–122.

40. Edgar Allan Poe, *The Fall of the House of Usher and Other Tales* (New York: The New American Library of World Literature, Inc., 1960). All quotations are from this edition.

41. *The Complete Poems of Emily Dickinson,* #1712, p. 696.

42. R. S. Thomas, "Silence" in *No Truce with the Furies* (Newcastle on Tyne: Bloodaxe Books, Ltd., 1995), p. 83.

43. Denise Levertov, "Suspended" in *The Stream and the Sapphire* (New York: A New Directions Book, New Directions Publishing Corporation, 1997), p. 24.

44. Isaac Rosenberg, "The Jew" in *Chapters into Verse: A Selection of Poetry in English Inspired by the Bible from Genesis through Revelation,* edit. Robert Atwan and Laurance Wieder (New York: Oxford University Press, 2000), p. 78.

45. Mark Twain, *The Adventures of Tom Sawyer,* (Chicago: A World Library Limited edition, Field Enterprises Educational Corporation, 1975). All quotations are from this edition.

46. A. N. Wilson, *Paul: The Mind of the Apostle* (New York: W. W. Norton and Company, 1997), pp. 230–231.

47. William Wordsworth, "Michael" in *Wordsworth: Selected Poetry,* edit. Nicholas Roe (New York: Penguin Books USA, 1992), p. 148.

48. *The Aeneid of Virgil,* trans. Allen Mandelbaum (New York: Bantam Books, 1971), p. 90.

49. Lewis Carroll, *The Annotated Alice: Alice's Adventures in Wonderland and Through the Looking Glass* (New York: Clarkson N. Potter, Inc., 1960). All quotations are from this edition.

50. *The Complete Poems of Emily Dickinson,* #341, p. 162.

51. Matthew Arnold, "Dover Beach" in *The Pocket Book of Verse* (New York: Pocket Books, Inc., 1940), p. 275.

52. "The Second Coming" in *Selected Poems and Two Plays of William Butler Yeats,* edit. M. L. Rosenthal (New York: Collier Books, Macmillan Company, 1966), p. 91.

53. "The Stare's Nest by My Window" in *Selected Poems and Two Plays of William Butler Yeats,* p. 107.

54. Nathaniel Hawthorne, *The House of Seven Gables* (New York: The Library of America, Literary Classics of the United States, Inc., 1983). All quotations are from this edition.

55. Charles Dickens, *David Copperfield* (New York: The Macmillan Company Division of the Crowell-Collier Publishing Company, 1962).

56. Charles Dickens, *Hard Times* (New York: Bantam Books, 1981). All quotations are from this edition.

57. *The Complete Poems of Emily Dickinson,* #149, p. 70.

58. James Joyce, *Ulysses* (New York: Vintage Books Division of Random House, 1986), p. 7.

59. *The Complete Poems of Emily Dickinson,* # 943, p. 441.

60. Isak Dinesen, "The Deluge at Norderney" in *Seven Gothic Tales* (New York: Random House, The Modern Library edition, 1934). All quotations are from this edition.

61. Thomas Helm, *Ordeal by Sea* (New York: New American Library Division of Penguin Putnam, Inc., 2001), p. 212–214.

62. Nathaniel Hawthorne, *The House of Seven Gables* (New York: The Library of America, Literary Classics of the United States, Inc., 1983). All quotations are from this edition.

63. Dylan Thomas, "Do Not Go Gentle into That Good Night" in *Collected Poems* (New York: New Directions Publishing Corporation, 1953).

About the Author

Geoff Wood holds a doctorate in theology and a licentiate in scripture from the Catholic University of America in Washington, D.C., and the Pontifical Biblical Institute in Rome. He is retired from an early academic career in religious studies and subsequent employment in the evaluation of human services at the national and local levels. Currently, he lives in Sonoma, California, where he continues to offer adult religious education courses at the parish and diocesan levels. He has been writing weekly essays for several California parishes since 1989.